Maureen,

MEMORIES OF

Forest View Gardens

Trudie Seybold

*Love
Trudie*

Dedicated to
the Memory of

Jennie and Karl Klose

Jay Russell

and

My Beloved Kurt

Cover paintings of Rottenburg an der Tauber by Jim Slouffman. Jim painted the murals for Forest View Gardens, and when we closed the restaurant, the murals were removed and we donated them to the Kolping German Society on Mills Road in Mt. Healthy.

Printed in the United States of America

First Printing, 2017

ISBN 978-1-945091-32-2

Ordering Information: Special discounts are available on quantity purchases by bookstores, corporations, associations, and others. For details, contact the publisher at:

    sales@braughlerbooks.com
    or at 937-58-BOOKS

For questions or comments about this book, please write to:

    info@braughlerbooks.com

Braughler™
Books
braughlerbooks.com

Contents

Introduction

The beginnings of Forest View Gardens are indelibly intertwined with my childhood. Let us turn the pages of history and cross the threshold of a charming adventure story.

I believe it was 1932 when my father invented a whirlpool for President Franklin D. Roosevelt, who had polio. We had moved to Washington, DC, and Mother tells me that when I was three or so, I was dancing with the Marine Band in front of the Capital. We later returned to Cincinnati and my father worked at Seagram Distillery in Lawrenceburg, Indiana. Mama and Daddy were born in 1898 and came from Germany in 1925. She brought her three brothers, a sister Zandel (Anna), her sister's baby, Ray, and her mother, Anna. For a time, my mother worked as an upstairs girl for the Goodrich family in Cottage Hills.

Daddy and Mama met at the Citizenship House and eventually married. Mother was born in Augsburg, Bavaria, and then moved to Biberach on der Reis. Mama told me that she lived in Biberach's Glocken Loch. My Dad was from the Rheinpfalz area.

In 1976, Luciano had sung in East Germany for the Handel Festival with the Promusica Society. We traveled on the Romantische Strasse and finally visited Biberach. My mother's description of things was always hilarious. I wanted to visit my mother's homestead, so we stopped in a little store and I said to the sales gal, "Können Sie Mir sagen woh ist das Glocken Loch (bell hole)?" She replied, "Sie sagt Wir haben keinen Loch aber Wir haben eine Glocken Gasse," which is Bell Alley. (*Glocken* is a bell in German.) There we found the homestead, a charming half-timber house with an enormous overhang. A neighbor came out and said that she remembered my mother.

When Mama and Daddy first came to America, they bought a house on McMicken Avenue, one block from McMillan. I was born on November 25, 1929. We had boarders, and in 1939, my father's mother came for a visit from the Rhineland. Karolina Klos, my precious grandmother, had lived all her life on a farm in Hütschenhausen. Poor *Grossmutter* couldn't go back home because of the war, so she stayed with us until 1941. Since we had both grandmothers living with us, I became an expert in the German language, and when Mama took me to Haberle Elementary School for Kindergarten, the teacher told Mama I would be maladjusted the rest of my life. However, I learned English quickly and am happy to be bilingual. After kindergarten, I attended Sacred Heart Catholic School in Camp Washington and started my piano studies with a wonderful nun by the name of Sr. Charles Louise. The nuns belonged to the Franciscan Order which is located in Oldenburg, Indiana.

In 1935, my father rented a garage for his car on Central Parkway, below a magnificent Victorian home located on McMicken Avenue. The house belonged to the Dewald family. The parents, who were also German, had passed away leaving behind five children, none of whom ever married. There were two sons and three daughters: Tante (we called a friend "Aunt" instead of "Miss") Erna, Tante Lenorie, and Tante Cornelia. I never met their brothers. These three ladies were such an inspiration to me as I was growing up. Tante Erna was such an artist, and in the tower room, she used to gild book bindings with gold. They were excellent cooks and prepared the best foods on a wood-burning stove. Tante Lenore taught German in the public schools until the turn of the 20th century, and Tante Cornelia worked in Washington, DC, for the government.

The Dewald's home was full of magnificent antiques, gorgeous marble mantel fireplaces in every room, glorious hardwood parquet floors, and original paintings. My favorite antiques were the bronze statuary. Fortunately, Tante Erna gave all the statuary to my mother and dad, and I have these beautiful figurines in my apartment. My favorite statue is one of Minerva, which stands on my treasured marble ironwork table made by my dad. The marble table is graced by a magnificent artistic iron-worked mirror, also made by my daddy.

We moved from McMicken to Monfort Heights shortly thereafter. After I had gone to Sacred Heart Catholic School since the first grade, my mother suggested I try Monfort Heights Elementary Public School. This adventure lasted just a few days when I convinced my mother to send me to St. Martin's of Tours School in Cheviot.

When I was in the fifth grade at St. Martins, Sister recommended that I advance my piano training with Mrs. Stoltzenbach Paine, then for a short time with Fred Noah, timpanist of the Cincinnati Symphony Orchestra, from Dresden, Germany. I studied with Mr. Noah until I attended Western Hills High School. My last teacher before graduating from high school was Leo Paalz, a piano teacher in the preparatory division of the old Conservatory of Music at Highland and Oak Streets. I loved Mr. Paalz; he was a great technician . While at Western Hills, I majored in music and office practice. My great inspiration in choral music was my choral director, Willis Beckett. Willis was also organist and choir director at Westwood First Presbyterian Church and conducted the ensemble choir at CCM. Even though I had been a member of the Catholic Church for so many years, I was encouraged by Mr. Beckett to join the choir at Westwood First. I loved the minister, Reverend Emmette Moorhead, and joined the Youth Group of over 100 students and vets. The group was called the "Triple F," and we still meet once a year at the Western Hills Country Club for lunch.

Trudie in high school.

I had a lead role in the *My Maryland* musical at Western Hills High and played "TicoTico" with David Worth and the Western Hills Band Wagon. Our director, Andy Brady, was also a great inspiration to me.

I was supposed to graduate from Western Hills in 1948, but I accelerated and graduated in 1947. I attended Hughes High School for the graduating credits. I took typing and was awarded a prize for my speed of 135 words a minute. Now I type 135 mistakes.

But back to Forest View Gardens. I remember a very cold autumn day in November 1939 when we drove with Mrs. Klein, the real-estate lady. She was describing a hidden jewel at 4508 North Bend Road in Montfort Heights. A gentleman by the name of Mr. Philippe owned this building that housed a chicken dinner restaurant open only in the summer. He must have been a botanist because of his love of rare trees and flowers. I remember an enormous plot of lily of the valley, a most fragrant little flower. I would pick little bouquets of lily of the valley and sell them to our friends. The restaurant was a frame structure, on stilts, with sliding windows, no basement, no furnace, and no air conditioners. It appeared to be a summer-type camp. In the front of the property was a St. Louis-type duplex. It consisted of two identical apartments. Oh, yes: there was also a third-floor bedroom.

After many sleepless nights, my mother Jennie and my dad Karl had decided to take the plunge and gave the real estate lady an offer. An offer that she couldn't resist. My mother, an incredible cook, was easily convinced to begin a new venture with the restaurant, and my dad was excited to own his own business. He had been an artistic iron worker and coppersmith from the old country in the Rhineland area of Germany called Hütschenhausen (where he was born) near the Ramstein Air Base operated by the U.S., and when he first came to Cincinnati, he worked at Vulcan Copper & Supply Company located on Sycamore Avenue. I found out many years later that our most regular customer at the restaurant, Bruce Fields (deceased), also worked with my father.

Between the restaurant building and the duplex was a small building housing the kitchen. We started with the similar fare of chicken dinners, deliciously fried and then slowly oven baked. Remember, this was at the beginning of World War II. Lots of items were rationed. But my dad, a farmer at heart, and originally from the Rhineland, bought several more acres of land from a Mr. Menzi. Then he acquired a Guernsey milk cow so we had all our own milk, butter, and cream. We also bought live chickens. Mama would slit their necks and plunge them into boiling water, and I would pluck the feathers. (I heard today that they have made an electric feather plucker!)

In 1941, we renamed the restaurant Forest View Gardens. My dad was busy remodeling the interior and excavating the basement so we could install a coal-burning furnace. Mama always called this rustic basement "Mammoth Cave."

The growth of the restaurant took place the day a gentleman knocked at our door and introduced himself as Dr. William Huebener, who reportedly had been the doctor for Kaiser Wilhelm of Germany. Dr. Huebener had an office on Park Avenue in East Walnut Hills. He loved the restaurant and encouraged my mother to venture into German cooking. Dr. Huebener, his wife Verna, and friends such as Judge Dammarell joined him for dinner at our restaurant. The doctor was a lover of the circus and of opera. He boarded two Ringling Brothers circus horses named Chico and King at the Westfork riding stables, and on Sundays, would ride the horses though Mt. Airy Forest to our restaurant. Mama made German Pancakes (crepes) and German pastries, including the best *schnecken* ever. The doctor enjoyed eating in the outdoor gazebo, named in his honor.

Not only did Dr. Huebener ride through the forest but he also would Roman Ride, standing on two horses and riding in circles at the stables. A memorable occasion was a visit of Felix von Luckner, the "Sea Devil" of the German Navy during World War I. He was accompanied by his great-grandnephew, Herman Luckner (deceased), and we

Dr. Huebener Roman riding.

entertained them in the old duplex on North Bend Road. I remembered playing *"Stille Nacht, Heiliege Nacht"* ("Silent Night") on the piano and singing it in German, so it must have been during the Christmas season.

The doctor's love for the circus was memorable. He once brought Karl Wallenda the high-wire artist whose great grandson, Nic, had recently walked over the Grand Canyon, etc., and I was his guest to all the Ringling Brothers circus events. I sang "Gia Nia Mia" which was played during their high-wire acts, so Dr. Huebener suggested I join the circus. I often wondered where I would have been singing with the circus. By the time you read this book, Ringling Bros. and Barnum & Bailey Circus will have closed for good (May, 2017.)

I graduated from the University of Cincinnati College-Conservatory of Music in May of 1951. My degree was a Bachelor in Music Education with a piano, voice, and choral directing major. I studied piano with Alma Betcher, Karin Dayas, and Mary Young in Accompanying; I studied voice with Laura May Wright (wife of Parvin Titus), Robert Powell, and Demetrie Onafrey. My mentors at the time were Willis Beckett and Larry Willhide. Sarah Yancy Cline was head of the Music Education department. I enjoyed all the German instrumentalists such as Hans Moesser, Henry Wholegmuth, and many others. The old Conservatory was located at Highland and Oak Streets. I was a member of Sigma Alpha Iota, Professional Music Fraternity. My mother catered several SAI parties and it was a lot of fun.

Before leaving Cincinnati, I sang "Die Macht der Musik" at Music Hall with William Kappelhof (Doris Day's father) and the German singing society with the Symphony.

My first teaching position in public school music was at Granby Elementary School in Forest Park, Norfolk, Virginia. I chose Norfolk because it was the home of Agnes (Meloni) Forte (deceased), my closest friend was a piano major at CCM. Agnes' family was Italian, and they were precious friends. I loved teaching, and organized a mini choir called the Klosetet. I directed *Amahl and the Night Visitors* by Carlos Menotti. I lived in a small house on Willabe Spit, close to the Naval Air Force Base. Outside of school, I was organist at Ocean View Presbyterian Church and sang arias from the *Marriage of Figaro* by Mozart with the Norfolk Symphony Orchestra, directed by Maestro Schenkman. I studied voice with Bertha Nelson, an incredible voice teacher. In the summer, I studied voice with Floyd Worthington at Carnegie Hall in New York City.

I finally decided to come home one summer and became reacquainted with my old boyfriend, James Barbour "Barb" Russell, III. We began dating. Barb was originally from Maysville, Kentucky, where the Russells were a very prominent family. Maysville has the famous movie theatre The Russell Theatre, built by his grandfather, J. Barbour Russell. Barb and I had met in summer school at UC. He was drafted and joined the Air Force. He enrolled in the Air Force Academy and was stationed near San Antonio, Texas. I joined him there, and we were married in Cincinnati on August 1, 1953. We decided to move to Coral Gables, Florida, where his father and second wife lived in the Redlands. His mother lived in Hyde Park and was married to Tony Shebanek; they had two boys, Ron and Tony. His father and wife Carolyn had three children: Babs, Robert, and Bill.

When we first arrived in Miami, we lived in an apartment on Douglas Avenue and eventually moved into a beautiful home in the Gables. My first teaching position was in the Redlands, south of Miami and the last city before the Keys. The Redlands consisted of many migrant workers, but I organized a great choir and enjoyed working with these students.

After the Redlands, I taught at Ponce de Leon Junior High and had a great group of students. Then I taught at Miami Jackson Senior High, where I produced *Rose Marie*. I believe they had a sign at the refugee center in downtown

Miami which advertised "Gertrude Klose Russell free voice lessons." While in Miami, Dr. Howard Doolin brought to our home a fabulous tenor from Cuba who was attending Coral Gables High School and sang in the choir with Jaunita Raefield. They produced *South Pacific* and Luciano Moral from Pinar del Rio, Cuba, one of my voice students, sang the role of Emile de Beck even though it was a baritone role. He was on a scholarship with me, and in exchange for his lessons, he moved into our home and took care of the yard and household tasks. Luciano was only sixteen, but a beautiful person and great musician. He was also soloist at Riviera Presbyterian Church where I was Minister of Music. I had six choirs and two hand bell choirs. My organist was Tom Evans (deceased).

Luciano and I were featured in the Spanish edition of *Life Magazine*, but he was not the only tenor from Cuba who studied with me. There was Enrique Monnar, Arturo de Castro, and Cesar Suarez. Cesar ventured into a musical career and sang with Joan Sutherland at the Michigan Opera Theater many years later in *I Puritani*. We drove to Michigan and enjoyed the production. He was also guest soloist at one of our galas to raise money for our CCM Scholarships. Unfortunately, Cesar passed away shortly after the affair.

Luciano and I sang in the Miami Opera Company under the direction of Arturo Di Fellippe in the opera *Samson and Delilah* with Sandra Warfield and James MacCracken. Luciano had a minor role as a messenger. We were also in

Left to right: David Goodman, Jack Frost,
Susan Gonzales.

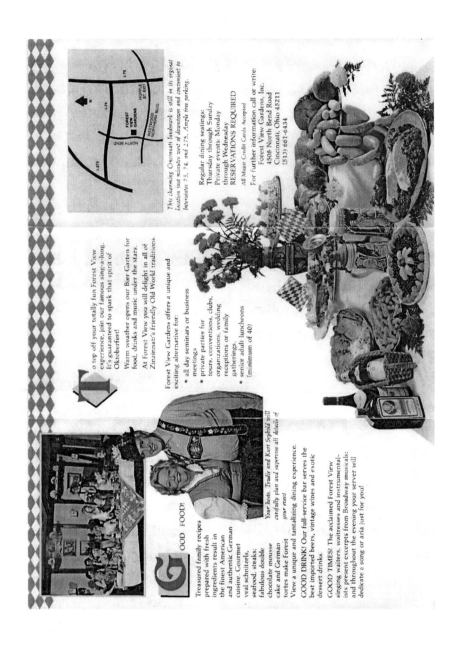

This charming Cincinnati landmark is still in its original location but mistakes west of downtown and convenient to Interstates 75, 74, and 275. Ample free parking.

Regular dining seatings:
Thursday through Sunday
Private events: Monday
through Wednesday
RESERVATIONS REQUIRED

All Major Credit Cards Accepted

For further information call or write:
Forest View Gardens, Inc.
4508 North Bend Road
Cincinnati, Ohio 45211
(513) 661-6434

To top off your totally fun Forest View experience, join our famous sing-a-long. It's guaranteed to spark that spirit of Oktoberfest!

Warm weather opens our Bier Garten for food, drinks and music under the stars.

At Forest View you will delight in all of Zinzinnati's friendly Old World traditions.

Forest View Gardens offers a unique and exciting alternative for:

- all day seminars or business meetings
- private parties for tours, conventions, clubs, organizations, wedding receptions or family gatherings
- senior adult luncheons (minimum of 40)

Your hosts, Trudis and Kurt Siegheld will carefully plan and supervise all details of your event.

G OOD FOOD!

Treasured family recipes prepared with fresh ingredients result in the finest American and authentic German cuisine. Gourmet veal schnitzels, seafood, steaks; fabulous double chocolate mousse cake and German tortes make Forest View a unique and tantalizing dining experience.

GOOD DRINK! Our full-service bar serves the best imported beers, vintage wines and exotic dessert drinks.

GOOD TIMES! The acclaimed Forest View singing waiters, waitresses and instrumentalists present excerpts from Broadway musicals; and throughout the evening your server will dedicate a song or aria just for you!

Aida with Nicola Moscona and Franco Correlli. Luciano also sang with Monseratte Cabelle and his favorite soprano, Joan Sutherland, in *Lakme.*

My last teaching job was at Coral Park Senior High. I directed several choirs at Coral Park, with my favorite being the Boys Choir. One of the members, Norman Weiss, has a great career, later conducting *Phantom of the Opera* on Broadway. My supervisor was Dr. Howard Doolin, who respected my vocal work.

Barbour and I had two boys. J. Barbour Russell IV born April 21, 1955, at Coral Gables Hospital, and Edward Allen Russell was born March 27, 1960, in the same hospital. Both boys were the love of my life.

When Luciano graduated from high school, he won a scholarship to study at Aspen Music Festival in Colorado. He sang the arias from *The Messiah*, by Handel, "Comfort Ye and Every Valley" It was incredible! His coloratura was glorious. My mother and I took the boys out to Aspen to be in attendance. It was a summer to remember. We stayed in the home of Luciano's sponsor, Mrs. Sweeny. Luciano studied with Roland Hayes, John McCullem, and Jennie Tourel, and had the lead role in the opera arranged by the artist in residence that summer, Darius Milhaud, *Robin and Marian.* Madame Milhaud helped Luciano with diction.

While Luciano was at Aspen, he applied to attend either Curtis Institute in Philadelphia or Julliard in New York. He selected Curtis and studien on scholarship with Madame Gregory.

By this time I had divorced Barbour due to differences in our beliefs and lifestyle in general. Jay had developed Juvenile Diabetes at the age of ten, and he led a difficult life with this disease. I was an active volunteer for JDF. When the Clooneys featured a Diabetes Gala at Music Hall featuring George, Rosie, and Nick, Dr. First (Jay's doctor) was at the party. Jay had a double transplant, kidney and pancreas, in 1994. He had ten years of a good life, suffered a bladder infection, they pumped him with antibiotics, and he died in 2003 at the tender age of 49. Eddie planned a burial service in Florida on a yacht because Jay loved the ocean and Florida.

Jay and his wife Susie had a beautiful daughter, Lacy, who is a cardiologist nurse in Florida, and a set of handsome twin boys: Jason, a tile setter and professional surfer, and Christopher, an artistic iron worker inspired by my dad. Chris has two adorable children: Jillian, 10 years old going on 30, and Christopher Bryan, 7.

Eddie and Lori live in Odessa, Florida. They had two daughters: Dermatology Dr. Nicole and Michael Howe have a baby boy, Quade; and Kelly and Michael Rothman, with baby girl Isa Bella. Eddie is the proud owner of Viage Group Boat dealership in Sarasota. Lori minds their home in Odessa, with several horses and a Doberman dog, name Zeus. Both are enjoying grandparent-hood.

Eddie was five when I ventured with Luciano to Philadelphia. I enrolled my name and experience with the Philadelphia School Board and immediately was hired as a choral director of Kensington Senior High School for Girls. I worked with Mardia Melroy, also a choral director. I really didn't enjoy Kensington High School, where I was selected to create a new type of learning experience. It was called "ES' 70" by a gentleman named Mr. Love. We ended up writing curriculum for a year relating music to math, science, art etc. It was a magnet school, in west Philadelphia. We finally opened the school for grades nine through twelve, and the principal was Dr. Davis B. Martin. I had a piano tech lab, the students and faculty were on a first-name basis, but we lost the funding and it turned out to be just another inner city high school.

I enjoyed my choirs, and the orchestra which was directed by Dan Panchelli. We made a perfect team. I was assistant choir director to Dr. Wendell Pritchett, who directed The All-City Choir. I enrolled at Temple University for my Masters in Music Ed where I worked with Robert Page (deceased) and graduated in 1973.

Luciano loved eighteenth-century architecture and furniture, and so did I. When we moved to Center City, I was free during the summer months, so I ran the food concession in the Rittenhouse Swim Club. We prayed for rainy days. My *blintzes* became famous. I finally moved out to the suburbs, to Wyncote, Pennsylvania. Eddie was enrolled at Wyncote Elementary School and Jay was at Cheltenham Senior High School.

While in Philly, I enhanced my salary by catering Cuban *empanitas*, a delicious Spanish meat turnover. I sold them to the Cheese Corner, a specialty shop in Germantown, Pennsylvania. Sometimes I would make at least four to five dozen all at a once, which was time consuming. I had met a lovely woman in Wyncote, Laura Nester, who made miniature quiche for the same company. Laura was a widow and a charming friend, with five children. She now lives in Sommerset, Pennsylvania.

I produced several musicals with Dan at Kensington High School. We did a fun *Promises, Promises,* and my farewell production was a fabulous Bernstein's *West Side Story.* I trained the football teams as Jets and Sharks; they were terrific and sounded good vocally.

That production was my swan song. My parents in Cincinnati wanted to retire, and my mother had to have hip surgery. I resigned my position and packed up a U-Haul. Luciano stayed in Philly on scholarship to Academy Vocal Arts, studying with Nicolo Moscona, Maestro Anton Guadagnio, and Tito Capobianco, who gave Luciano his pet Collie from Argentina, named Gaucho. Luciano sang the role of Hadji in *Lakme* with Joan Sutherland.

In 1976, Luciano sang with the ProMusica Society directed by Dr. Zimmerman, and they flew to Germany for the Handel International Festival in Halle, Germany. They also sang in Dresden, Berlin, and other East German cities. After the concerts were over, I met him in Frankfort and we rented a car, drove from Heidelberg through the Romantische Strasse to Bavaria, even to my mother's hometown of Biberach an der Reis, and to the charming Black Forest.

After I moved back to Cincinnati so my parents could retire, I decided to hire Greman-speaking students in the restaurants. One evening, a customer wanted to speak to me. Hal Lassiter, Dean of Admissions at CCM, spoke a little German since he had been stationed during the war near Ramstien, Germany. He asked about hiring some of the opera singers as waiters and waitresses, as I had done. That was the beginning of the greatest venture. We placed a notice on the activity board in the CCM lounge, and the applications were many. I also needed pianist and arrangers for mini productions of musicals. One day an accordionist dropped by. He said, "What you need is an accordionist that's Irish, but looks German." That was Jack Frost, a fabulous musician. We chose a young high school student named Teddy Babst to join him on the drums. Jack and Teddy worked for us until we closed. Jack now resides in Liberty Nursing Home of Colerain Township.

Martha Crabtree at CCM gave me a room to rehearse the singers. My first musical arranger was Doug Pennington. He arranged a group of musicals that were just fabulous. He was famous for our annual Festival of Carols, which I directed. Our first show was *Fiddler on the Roof* featuring friends of mine from CCM. Maurice Mandell was Tevia, and his wife, Louise Ruehlman Mandell, was Golde. Both of these artists graduated from CCM. Maurice was a great Buffo Bass and Louise was the sister of Eugene Ruehlman, who was mayor of Cincinnati. Needless to say, it was an incredible evening and production.

Doug also worked with me on *My Fair Lady*, *The Fantasticks* (with Kenny Benz), *South Pacific*, *The Student Prince*, *Rodgers and Hart Medley*, *Cole Porter Medley*, *Kismet*, *Carousel*, the famous *Christmas Medley*, *Oklahoma*, and *Jerome Kern/Porter Medley*. I encouraged Doug to have other arrangers such as Mathew Spady, Dr. Christina Haan (organist at Knox Pres.), and many other talented musicians arranged our thirty-minute shows. We had musicals from Gershwin, Berlin, Rodgers and Hammerstein's (*The Sound of Music* "Edelweiss" became our theme song), and of course Bernstein (*West Side Story*), Lerner and Loewe, (*Guys and Dolls* was written up in our *Cincinnati Enquirer*), *Fiddler on the Roof*, *Gigi*, *Brigadoon*, Andrew Lloyd Webber (*Cats*, *Phantom of the Opera*), and even Sondheim.

We usually had two seatings on Friday. Thomas Bankston, baritone, our first Professor Engel in the *Student Prince*, has been Artistic Director of the Dayton Opera Company for twenty years. Jeff Martin is singing in Germany. Helene Schneiderman has been an artist with the Heidelburg Opera and the Stuttgart Opera house for over thirty years. I remember going to the San Francisco Opera in 1994 to hear her in the *Barber of Seville* singing the role of Rosina with Paul Pliska, Nathan Gunn as Figaro, and Cathy Cook singing Bertha. Forest View was well represented that evening. Helene sang Baroness with the Santa Fe Opera in the summer of 2016, and in the Met debut as Annina in *Der Rossenkavalier* in April 2017. Hope we get it at the movies!

Other wonderful individuals who performed or played at Forest View Gardens include:

Dale Staley (deceased)

Danny Boggus (deceased)

Beth McVey (appeared on Broadway)

Walter Cuttino sang in Achen,

Lisa Griffith is an opera singer in Dortmond, Germany

Laura Lanham Frank

Monica Schanzer sings in Germany

Michael von Engen (deceased)

Bard Suverkrop sang in Germany

Thomas Haffner

Larry Alexander

Laurinda Nikkel

Mia Randell,

Laurie Wyatt is choral director at SCPA

Terry Hodges

Michael Rodgers

Joyce Bartels

Susan Benkin

Kathy Jennings

Chuck Frank

David Goodman

Kathy Branyon

Dawn Young

Barbara Fox

Janice Fulbright

Robert Claytor

Randy Locke

Carol Sparrow

Dale Ganz

Bob Ricketts

Steve Lusman

Carolann Mary

Victor Ciepiel

Francis McGill

Janet Lamb

Spring Pillow

Walter Poole (deceased)

Ron Baker

Nancy Love

Linda Laible

Georga Osborne

Susan Gonzalez is a professor at Hunter College in New York

Lincoln Chapman

Kirby Traylor

Peter Dunham

Marc Semrow (deceased)

Nancy Martin

Luctrician Booth

Dale Travis

Michael Sokol

Piotr Gajewski is a pianist

John Koch, baritone and artistic director of the Midwest Institute of Opera and professor nineteen years

Dr. Michelle Vought

Lora Fabio (Germany)

Tony Fabio (deceased)

David Small

Philip Horst

Shawn Tully

Jody Traver

Kate Healy

Tregoney Shepherd

Jennifer Carnahan

Reuvin Aristigieti

Timothy Swain

Jim Haffner

John Fowler

Eric Ashcraft

Kathleen Thompson

Randall Gremillion

Tom Commersford

Beth Gelsinger

Alex Koslovsky

Margie Oxley

Krisleah Schlender

Micah Graber

Lisa Shaw

Diana Cataldi

Richard Teaster

Christopher Fuller

Barbie MacCullam

Matt Schlommer

Karin Fraley

Jennifer Davidson

Daniel Mobbs

Catherine Cook

Mark Duffin

Jann Degnan

Titi Adedokun, Miss Ohio 1994 and who has an operatic career in Munich, Germany

Ryan Olsen

Kathleen Koon

Michael Koon

Diane Heldman

Peter Else

Sam Smith

Anthony Offerle

Kristen Claytor

Michael Moulder

Carole Latimer

William Park

Richard Zeller

Ross Stoner

Neal Harrelson

Renee Lawless, on Broadway

Stephanie Monsour

Robbie Hutson

Michael Hendricks

Richard Lewis

Joyce Bartels

Aaron Dalton,

Richard Lissimore

Michelle Felliciak

Timothy Schorr

Ana Rodriguez

Brenda Baker

Katrina Thurman

Richard Koons

James Lynn

David Moore

William Parsons

Kevin Augsberger

Aaron Dalton

Sinclair Mitchell

Ben Smith

Kelly Fox

Shannan Brock

Maria Ventura

Alison Acord (Dr and Prof. at Miami U.)

Andrew Garland

Jaclyn Kleier

Cincinnati Chorus

Daniel Keeling

Wayne Tigges

Megan Monogham

Alma Jean Smith

David Adam Moore (has a Met contract through 2017)

Lillian Valdez

Mathew Spady

Lutricia Booth

Sam Smith sang in Cincinnati Opera's *Tosca* in 2016.

Dan Okulith, baritone

Danny Mobbs

David Small

Victor Ciepiel and his wife, Mary opened Vito's Café in Ft. Thomas, Kentucky. His cuisine was Italian, with singers from CCM and Northern Kentucky University. It was a great restaurant, but no longer open.

Jim Abegglin,who is now living in Indian Rocks Beach on the west coast of Florida. He is Artistic Director of Performing Arts at the Royal Palm Retirement Community.

Thomas Hammons of Cincinnati has had a contract with the Met for over twenty years and now is freelancing. He is working throughout the US, presently singing in Omaha, and in our production of *Tosca* he will sing the role

Kurt and Trudi with mezzo-soprano Susan Quittmeyer and her
husband James Morris, a bass-baritone. Both Susan and James have
performed with the Metropolitan Opera.

of the Sacristan. I still remember his wonderful Dulcamara
in *Elixir of Love* in Canada.

Robbi Hutson, a wonderful Papagano in *The Magic
Flute* has developed into a project manager for the Hyatt
Hotels and Resorts in the Caribbean.

Scott Lawton, arranger of our *Miss Saigon*, lives and
has worked in Germany, and is married with two sons.
Scott has been conductor of the Landespoliz Orchestra for
twelve years in Nordheim-Westlen, and also conductor of
the Deusche Film Orchestra.

Dale Travis, bass, came to visit me in January 2017 with
his wife, Lisa and son Zach, who was auditioning at CCM,

for his Masters in Composition and French Horn. Dale used to perform as Elvis Presley, costume and all, for extra income.

• • •

Singers enchanted the customers and brought music and a friendly ambiance to our customers. Now, living at Evergreen Retirement Community, I assume that 85% of the residents know me as "Trudie of Forest View Gardens."

My father passed away in 1978 from heart failure, and we had a beautiful memorial service with the Hanselman Masonic Lodge in Clifton, and my future husband Kurt presiding.

Jennie and Karl Klose

Fabulous Eighties

My mother lived until 1984, and passed away from leukemia (blood cancer) on Mother's Day, with my son Jay at her side. Mother's Day always brought two seatings and a packed house. She was such a devoted mother and businesswoman. After retiring, her favorite job was to fold hundreds of napkins with Boo Reilling (grandmother of Teddy, our drummer.) She requested that in lieu of flowers, we would establish a scholarship at the CCM for promising singers.

My friend and insurance agent Kurt Seybold became my mentor and my lover. Kurt was married, but he needed my love and the challenge of the business. I needed him to help me with the financial end of things. We were married December 31, 1983. His friend and mentor, the Rev. Herman Helfrich, performed the ceremony with glorious music, food, and ambiance. We invited our friends, and the wedding party ended early so we could get our dining room ready for our annual New Year's Eve party and joyously welcome in the year 1984. Susan Gonzalez, Luciano, and Kenny Benz (deceased) provided a fabulous buffet.

Mother and Daddy had a beautiful house off of Hader Avenue situated on the twenty acres of land behind the restaurant. Kurt and I remodeled the beautiful brick home, adding a large bedroom with a Jacuzzi bathroom and a magnificent pool and pool house. The pool was great entertainment for our employees. We named the pool house "Karlsruhe" in memory of my father. This year as I am finishing my story, I celebrated my 32nd wedding anniversary, remembering my beloved Kurt who I miss more each day. My beloved partner passed away April 7, 2014 (obit from the *The Cincinnati Enquirer*, Jannelle Gelfand: "Kurt Seybold, 76, was a melodious host.")

SEYBOLD

Kurt, 76 beloved husband of Trudie Seybold, father of Sandy Seybold of Bonita Springs in Florida and his son, Kurt Gary deceased and step sons Eddie Russell, Jay Russell deceased , Luciano Moral and 5 grandchildren and 2 great grandchildren. He passed on April 7th, Kurt was born in Memmingen, Germany in 1937 and came to America in 1955. He became an American Citizen and pledged his love and loyalty to this country. He worked as an insurance salesman for Nationwide and then in 1978 joined Trudie at their successful restaurant, Forest View Gardens in Monfort Heights. He established an Opera Scholarship at the University of Cincinnati, CCM. He was an active member of Shriners International, The Grand Chapter of Royal Arch Masons of Ohio, Hanselmann Lodge, Knights Templar of Cincinnati and The Royal Order of Jesters, Court #7. He was a member of the Clifton Music Club, MacDowell Society of Cincinnati. He was involved in the development of School Creative Performing Arts. He was a life member of the Cincinnati Opera. Memorable donations in lieu of flowers can be sent to CCM Foundation at the University of Cincinnati to the Seybold/Russell/ Scholarship Fund, Cincinnati Opera Company, or Crossroads Hospice. Celebration of his life will be April 29th, on his birthday 7 P.M.-9 P.M. at Evergreen Retirement Community Auditorium, 230 West Galbraith Road, Cincinnati, Ohio 45215.

Kurt Seybold, 76, was a melodious host

By Janelle Gelfand
jgelfand@enquirer.com

Kurt Seybold would serenade his customers with a rendition of "My Way" with a Manhattan in his hand at the end of every evening at Forest View Gardens.

"To this day, when I hear 'My Way,' I think of Kurt before I think of Sinatra," said Titilayo Adedokun-Helm, the former Miss Ohio and Miss America runner-up, one of some 200 singers who got their start singing at the German restaurant in Monfort Heights.

Mr. Seybold, who owned Forest View Gardens with his wife, Trudie, before it closed in 2001, is remembered as a kind and generous man with a soft spot for singers. He loved life and always had time for a wicked joke or a good laugh.

He died April 7 of complications from congestive heart failure. He was 76.

Mr. Seybold

"In the early days, when I worked there, Kurt added a true sense of gemütlichkeit to the whole atmosphere," said Thomas Hammons, of Lebanon, a renowned bass-baritone who was a singing waiter as a University of Cincinnati College-Conservatory of Music student before debuting at the Metropolitan Opera. "We worked very hard on hot nights, and sweated and served sauerbraten and sang. Afterward, we went to the biergarten for a cold beer, to relax. It was

as though we were transported to Bavaria for an evening. None of us had ever experienced this kind of welcome before. This was the real thing."

"There was such a feeling of hospitality. Their door was always open to us, and they were always helpful in whatever way they could be," said singer and local voice teacher Lincoln Chapman, of Corryville, who sang at the restaurant for 10 years. "I first met Kurt at Oktoberfest, where he was singing on Fountain Square."

Trudie and Kurt Seybold said "auf wiedersehen" to their restaurant in 2001, ending a 62-year tradition of authentic German cooking that had begun with Trudie's mother, Jennie Klose. In the late '70s, Trudie Seybold introduced talented singers from CCM as waiters and waitresses, who served up arias and show tunes along with sauerkraut balls.

In 1978, Mr. Seybold walked into Forest View Gardens for the first time. His future wife, who had been working in the kitchen, noticed his "beautiful eyes and the most gorgeous voice." They began communicating. He soon asked the CCM graduate for voice lessons and, in 1984, her hand. They were married for 30 years.

Mr. Seybold hosted the shows, ran the business and kept the books meticulously.

"He just loved it," Trudie Seybold said. "He was the host, introducing people, because I was usually in the kitchen. Every night he joined in on the singing."

Mr. Seybold was born in 1937 in Memmingen, Germany. His father was killed by Russian soldiers right after World War II, and his mother died when he was 15. In 1955 at age 18, he emigrated to Cincinnati, sponsored by an aunt, and later became an American citizen.

His first job was at Kahn's (in the ham department) because he spoke no English and most of its employees were German. He worked as an insurance salesman for Nationwide for nearly 30 years.

Mr. Seybold shared his wife's love of opera, and the couple hosted cast parties for Cincinnati Opera for two decades.

"He had an outsized personality, which was truly operatic, and one of the things I always loved about him was his overflowing enthusiasm for anything in which he was involved, whether it was expressing a vivid opinion of what he'd just seen on the stage, or reliving a memory of Forest View Gardens, in his inimitable German accent," said Evans Mirageas, artistic director of Cincinnati Opera.

The couple has closely followed the careers of each of their singers. In 1987, they established the Klose-Seybold Memorial Scholarship at CCM in honor of their parents.

Later renamed the Seybold-Russell Scholarship Award, the prize is part of the school's annual opera scholarship competition.

Mr. Seybold was also an original member of a group involved in the development of the School for Cre-

ative and Performing Arts and helped to find the arts school's former home on Sycamore Street. He was active at the United Church of Christ, Shriners International, The Grand Chapter of Royal Arch Masons of Ohio, Hanselmann Lodge, Knights Templar of Cincinnati and The Royal Order of Jesters, Court #7.

On the final night that Forest View Gardens was open, June 2, 2001, Mr. Seybold stood for one last toast. But on this occasion, he changed the words of "My Way."

"He sang, 'And we did it our way,'" said his wife.

Some of the former singers from Forest View Gardens will participate in a celebration of his life from 7-9 p.m. Tuesday, Mr. Seybold's birthday, at Evergreen Retirement Community Auditorium, 230 West Galbraith Road, Hartwell.

Besides his wife, Mr. Seybold is survived by a daughter, Sandy Seybold, of Bonita Springs, Fla., step-sons Eddie Russell of Tampa and Luciano Moral of Augusta, Ky., five grandchildren and two great-grandchildren. A son, Kurt Gary Seybold, and stepson Jay Russell preceded him in death.

Memorial donations can be sent to the Seybold/Russell Scholarship Fund, UC College-Conservatory of Music External Relations Office, P.O. Box 210003, Cincinnati, OH 45221-0003; Cincinnati Opera, 1243 Elm St., Cincinnati, OH 45202; or Crossroads Hospice, 4380 Glendale-Milford Road, Cincinnati, OH 45242. ∎

My beloved Kurt.

Opera Parties

Beginning in 1978, Kurt and I had decided to sponsor an opera party each season. It was fun to invite the cast and board members

This is when Gus Stuhlreyer and Jim deBlasis were in charge, and finally, Nic Muni. Our opera parties were special, deluxe evenings with delicious food and drinks. Stars attending our parties included Italo Tajo, Charlotte Schockley, Richard Leech, Paul Plishka, Jim Morris, Randy Locke, Michael von Engen, Patricia Craig, Barbara Daniels, Tom Fox, John Fowler, Ed Fath, Steve Lusman, Tony Offerle, Jan Conrads, Carol Ann Mary Slouffman, Tracy Staver, Carol Sparrow, Barbara Fox, Cecily Nall, Diana Heldman, Jack Eddleman, Victoria Vagara, Johnny Alexander, Johanna Meier, Giorgio Tozzi, and many of our servers. We hosted several singers in our home during rehearsals, including Chen Ye (who was in *Nixon in China*), Mark Doss (an incredible bass), and our charming tenor, Scott Pieper.

Cooks, Management

I imagine you have been wondering: Who was cooking? Who was in charge of the schooling and rehearsal of the mini-shows?

When I first took over the restaurant, I was the executive chef. Mildred Battle and Tinnie B. Young were in charge of the kitchen, leftovers from my parent's rule. Unfortunately, Mildred was killed by her son for a pack of cigarettes. Tinnie stayed with me, and then Luciano decided to move to Cincinnati and help. Not only was Luciano a great singer but an excellent cook. He joined us in 1978 and became my head chef. He stayed with us until he opened his own charming Colonial restaurant, The Bee Hive Tavern located in Augusta, Kentucky, the home town of George Clooney and his parents. Luciano was made a Colonel and Admiral by the Governor of Kentucky, and his famous guest was the ever-popular Rosemary Clooney. Luciano owned this charming restaurant for twenty-five years. When he closed on Valentine's Day in 2013, he sang a beautiful Neopolitan song, accompanied by myself, with George Clooney a diner, and his family Nic and Nina. Luciano got a standing ovation.

One of our dishwashers, Billie McKenny, was training as our sous chef. He was most talented in decorating and cooking. We made all of our salad dressings, and all the recipes were authentically delicious. I will include some of our popular recipes at the end of my memoirs. Tiny was my yeast dough baker. She made the most delicious Hungarian finger torte which we would serve to rehearsal dinner guests or parties celebrating a special occasion. The dough was the same as the one for Schnecken, or in English, sticky buns. When Billie decided to open his own restaurant in Cheviot, we hired a talented cook, Ben Brown, from Nivas, Caribbean. Ben was most capable and stayed with us until we closed. While he was in control, Kurt and I decided to enhance the interior of the restaurant.

Forest View Expands

We decided to make it into a Bavarian-style restaurant. We spoke with Bruce Robinson Architecture Company and the Walter Hudepohl Construction Company, who fulfilled our dream. We enhanced the Bier Garden and added a smaller dining room, called the Edelwiess Room, open for lunch and smaller private parties. To make this room look truly Bavarian, we hired a Cincinnati artist and husband of one of our singers, Jim Slouffman. Jim painted two beautiful murals of Rottenburg an der Tauber. When we closed the restaurant in 2001, a German craftsman removed the murals from the wall and we donated them to the Kolping German Society which is located on Mills Road in Mt. Healthy. Carolann Mary directs the Kolping Choir.

Kurt typically had a traditional sing-a-long. Everyone was sitting at long tables, where they could swing arm-in-arm. His songs were "O Due Lieber Augustin," "The Happy Wanderer," "Du, du, Liegst mir in Herzen," "Edelweiss," "In München stedt ein Hofbriehaus," and "Lili Marlene."

The room graced the bar, Bier Garden, and newly-built restrooms. The foyer displayed the pictures of our singers and German steins and décor. We constantly concerned

New 75-seat addition to Forest View Gardens --
an indoor Bier Garten!

Artist's rendering of the Edelweiss room at Forest View Gardens.

ourselves with the customers' comfort while waiting for the seatings to begin, and the weather was also a great concern. Jim Slouffman is now president of The Wagner Society of Cincinnati.

Needless to say, the *Cincinnati Enquirer* was impressed and many positive articles were written by Jim Knippenberg (deceased) and Ray Cooklis. Ray's article was a sensational story "Schnitzel Und Opera." "At Forest View Gardens, servers sing for your supper." Pictures included the servers in their German-style dirndls: Lynda Keith serving salad after singing an aria, then Lynda joining Ron Baker in the drinking song from Romberg's *Student Prince*. Lincoln Chapman, glorious tenor and teacher at Vocal Arts and

Good Food ◆ Good Drink ◆ Good Times

EDELWEISS BIER STUBE
and outdoor Bier Garten

Zinzinnati's world famous Bavarian-style restaurant where it's always Oktoberfest!
4508 North Bend Road ◆ Cincinnati, Ohio 45211 ◆ (513) 661-6434

Flyer showing Edelweiss Room, with the original locations of
Jim Slouffman's Rothenberg murals (as seen on the cover).

SCPA, was known to sing a wonderful "Old Man River"
even though it was always sung by a bass. Nancy Love, Rich
Lissimore, Lucricia Booth, and many more enjoyed singing.

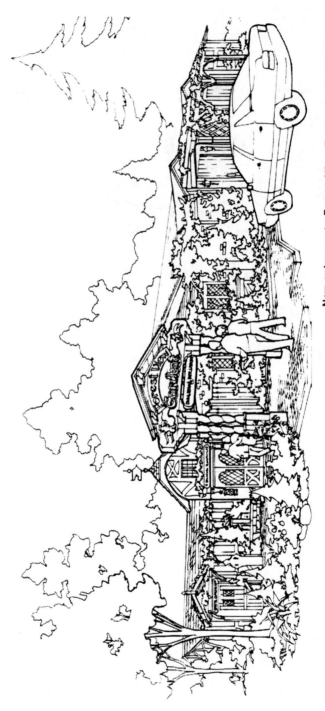

New entrance to Forest View Gardens. Main dining room at right, new indoor Bier Garten at left.

Trudie and Kurt Seybold, owners of Forest View Gardens, stand before their newly-remodeled restaurant/showplace. More than $500,000 worth of renovations were performed on the establishment at 4508 North Bend Road.

Gardens' growth now completed

Trudie Seybold has always thought of Forest View Gardens as "the showplace of Cincinnati." Now, because of more than half a million dollars worth of recent renovations, even more patrons can experience the mix of music and food at the Monfort Heights establishment, 4508 North Bend Road.

Seybold and her husband, Kurt, have waited patiently while construction workers labored to make the following changes: construction of a 75-seat bier garten, a new bar, completely remodeled restrooms, a new cathedral-ceilinged foyer and expansion of the main dining room.

"Our faithful guests who come early for their seatings will no longer be inconvenienced by an outside wait," Kurt said. "This expansion is a long-awaited dream for us."

Both say the recent renovations will enhance "the informal environment" of the musical restaurant, which features ex-

cerpts from Broadway shows sung by the waiters and waitresses, all of whom are trained operatic talents.

"It really is a unique place," Trudie said. "Good food, good times. It's hard work, but the people enjoy it. We have very good customers."

The addition of the beer garden makes expanded hours possible. The Seybolds have added Monday-Friday luncheons in the bier garten, which will also be open Thursday to Sunday, from 5-10 p.m.

The new and expanded establishment represents the Seybold's philosphy behind their work. Kurt explains:

"If you love what you're doing, you can achieve success," he said. "And we love what we're doing."

The restaurant is also open for private parties Monday and Tuesday. For more information, or to make reservations, call 661-6434.

We could seat 180 legally and usually had eight singers per show and seating. During the Christmas season, we
also had a seating in the Edelweiss Room, using four more
singers and a pianist. Each evening, we opened the seating
with "Wilkommin" from *Cabaret*. Kurt would introduce
our guests with special announcements and then introduce
the singers. Everyone joined in to sing all the Oktoberfest
songs. All of our customers sat at long tables so they could
swing and sway with one another and sing the famous German folk songs.

Our singers enjoyed entertaining our guests. We con-
cluded the evening with a sing-along, the "Chicken Dance,"
and then highlights from a Broadway musical. One of our
terrific basses created a "Strudel" song in honor of Trudie.
Ben Brown, our chef, would make two enormous strudels on
a serving tray, and when they were golden brown, the fabulous bass Aaron Dalton brought out the whole tray and sang:

The Strudel Song

Chorus: Bring back my strudel to me to me (Repeat)

My visit to old Zincinnat
Was ganz ausgezeihnet, it's true!
So here I am at Forest View

Chorus

I sit myself down with the menu
Get sauerkraut balls and chablis
So glücklich to knowi that for Nachtisch
Some strudel is waiting for me!

Chorus

I eat all my schnitzeli mit späzle,
The show it was.... It was alright
And yet without fresh apple strudel
I just can't call it a night

Chorus

My waitress brings out the dessert tray
With chocolate mousse and cheese cake
(Falsetto) "I'm sorry, we're all out of strudel,
It takes a few hours to bake"

The piano or accordion played a V7th chord, the kitchen door opened, and Trudie entered with a tray of oven baked strudel! Everyone sings:

She brought back, brought back,
she brought back my strudel to me, to me!
Brought back brought back,
brought back my strudel to me!

Amen and thanks Aaron Dalton.

KURT'S TRADITIONAL SING-A-LONG
(arr. John G. Banner, Esq.)

O, du lieber Augustin

O, du lieber Augustin,
Augustin, Augustin,
O, du lieber Augustin
   Alles ist hin!

Geld ist weg, Mensch ist weg
Alles ist hin, Augustin!
O, du lieber Augustin,
   Alles ist hin!

The Happy Wanderer

I love to go a-wandering
Along the mountain track
And as I go, I love to sing
My knapsack on my back. *

I wave my hand to all I meet,
And they waive back to me,
And blackbirds call
So loud & sweet
From ev'ry green wood tree. *

Chorus:

*Val-deri, Val-dera,
Val-deri,
Val-dera-ha-ha-ha-ha-
Val-deri, Val-dera, my
Knapsack on my back.

Du, du, liegst mir im Herzen

Du, du, liegst mir im Herzen, Du, du, liegst mir im Sinn
Du, du, macht mir viel Schmerzen
Weiss nicht wie gut ich dir bin!
* Ja, Ja, Ja, Ja!
Weiss nicht wie gut ich dir bin! (*Repeat Ja, Ja)

Edelweiss
Edelweiss, Edelweiss, every morning you greet me
Small and white, clean and bright,
You look happy to meet me.

*Blossom of snow may you bloom and grow,
Bloom and grow forever. Edelweiss, edelweiss
Bless my homeland forever. (*Repeat chorus)

Song sheets from the restaurant.

42

Lili Marlene

Vor der Kaserne,
Vor dem grossen Tor,
Stand eine Laterne,
Und steht sie noch davor,
So woll'n wir uns da wieder sehen
Bei der Laterne wollen wir stehen
Wie einst, Lili Marlene,
Wie einst, Lili Marlene!

Underneath the lantern by the barrarck gate
Darling I remember the way you used to wait,
'Twas there that you whispered tenderly
That you loved me
You'd always be,
My Lili of the lamplight,
My own Lili Marlene!

Auf Wiedersehen Sweetheart

Auf wiedersehen, auf wiedersehen,
We'll meet again, sweetheart.
This lovely day, has flown my way
The time has come to part,
We'll kiss again, like this again
Don't let the teardrops start,
With love that's true, I'll wait for you
Auf wiedersehen, sweetheart!
(Repeat Entire Verse)

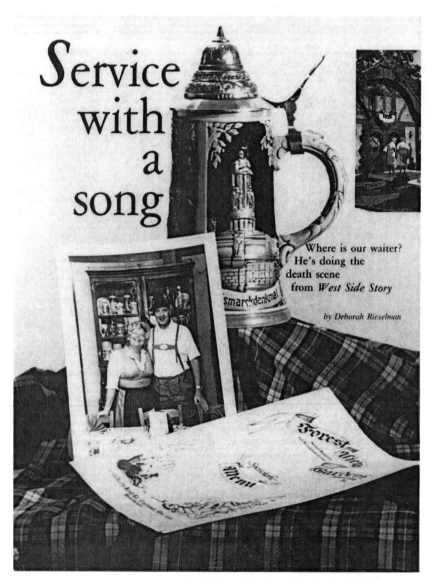

Service with a song

Where is our waiter? He's doing the death scene from *West Side Story*

by Deborah Rieselman

From the University of Cincinnati's "Horizons" article,
October 1988

Opposite page: A picture of Trudie and Kurt Seybold in their best German attire rests against a German beer stein. Above, from left to right: Guests arrive at the newly redecorated Forest View Gardens. Servers Eric Ashcraft and Maria Ventura serenade each other and their customers. Lincoln Chapman delivers food before delivering his song.

O ver the fields came the figure of a man riding two horses, standing up, with one foot astride each back. Roman riding it was called. Gertrude Klose knew the term as well as any circus performer. Although the mode of travel was certainly one of the flashiest ways to come to her parents' restaurant, it was not a new way. It had been done before. Bareback riders, along with other circus stars like Emmett Kelly and the flying Wallendas, were often guests at Forest View Gardens.

Such was the atmosphere in which "Trudie" Klose Seybold grew up— hobnobbing with celebrities, not only circus greats, but international dignitaries and opera stars. It was a colorful crowd to serve and an impressive crowd to entertain. And she did both, thanks to William Heubener.

Heubener, who once was Kaiser Wilhelm's personal physician, was responsible for much of what happened in Trudie's life. It was at his insistence that her mother, Jennie Klose, opened the restaurant in 1940. It was with his encouragement that Trudie started singing and playing piano for restaurant patrons. Furthermore, it was his love of throwing parties that popularized the restaurant among celebrities.

But most important, it was Heubener's lingering influence that led Gertrude Klose Seybold to turn the restaurant into a Bavarian showplace in the '70s. Since that day, she has been helping to launch CCM's top operatic students into world-renowned careers.

Even though Trudie had grown up serving and entertaining illustrious restaurant customers, as a young adult she wanted to make a living

far from kitchens. Apparently the lure of teaching and coaching music was stronger than that of killing and cleaning chickens before her performances.

Music had always been a passion. Besides Heubener's parties, she had been involved in music lessons, school choruses, and church choirs—all advocated by her mother, who loved music with equal enthusiasm. When Trudie decided to enter the Cincinnati Conservatory and the University of Cincinnati, no one was surprised. In 1951, she graduated with two degrees—one in voice and one in music education.

She began her career in Norfolk, Virginia, singing with the symphony and earning recognition as one of the state's most creative music teachers. Two years later she moved to Miami, where she directed ten choirs at one church, coached opera members, served as choral director of the county school system, and developed Dade County Opera Company's first school program.

The job that most tugged at her heart, however, was one for which she accepted no pay: working as a voice coach for Cuban refugees. In 1964, she became the legal guardian of one of her Latin-speaking proteges, and Luciano Morale officially became one of the family, along with her other sons, Jay and Eddie.

Despite the rewards of her Florida career, the urge for change brought her to Philadelphia in 1968. There she became assistant choral director of the Philadelphia All-City Choirs, wrote a music curriculum for an alternative school, taught private students, and received a master's in music education from Temple University.

Her sights did not focus on Forest View Gardens again until 1975, when her parents decided to retire. With little commitment to the long term, Trudie took a leave of absence from her job to try her hand at running the business.

At the time, her parents had been operating the restaurant as a private facility for banquets and weddings. Trudie maintained the same approach, but did not like it. Fortunately, before she had made any decisions regarding in which direction to head next, she met UC College-Conservatory of Music Assistant Dean Hal Laster.

The two were comparing stories about people and places they both had known when Trudie recalled

From left to right: Maria Ventura sings happy birthday to Larry Habig, who had turned 103 and who later did a birthday dance on stage. Opening-show entertainment includes a few songs by Kirby Traylor, Alison Acord, Eric Ashcraft, and Laurie Wyandt.

Above: Jack Frost, "the Irish accordionist who looks German," leads the crowd in a beer chugging song.

how she used to play and sing for Forest View guests. Suddenly, the concept seemed ripe to try again—having waiters and waitresses entertain the guests. Laster suggested hiring CCM opera and musical theater graduate students.

To try out the idea, Trudie enlisted two old friends, Louise Mandell, CCM '49, MEd '71, EdD '74, and her husband, Maurice, CCM '49 and '71, who performed excerpts from *Fiddler on the Roof* in exchange for their meals. The show was such a success that Trudie followed it with *Cabaret*, *The Student Prince*, and *The King and I.*

Those shows remain among her most popular, although she has nearly forty that rotate monthly. At any one time, she maintains a staff of about twenty-two singing servers. Most work for three or four years, while completing their education.

Servers must attend rehearsals, report to work an hour before the first seating, then wait on customers in between performances on the restaurant's tiny stage....Or do they perform on stage in between waiting on customers? It's hard to tell.

Somehow they manage to take orders and serve cocktails and appetizers before singing an opening act. Then while taking entree orders and serving salads, they individually sing a variety of songs, anything from pop to light opera. After entrees are served, they join in on sing-alongs and polkas. Finally, as desserts make it to the tables, they change into costumes for the evening's Broadway show. Afterwards, they change back into their Bavarian-style uniforms, handle diners' checks, and make change.

Believe it or not, the juggling becomes "second nature," Trudie swears. "Only one in two hundred find they really can't do it."

Richard Zeller, MM '88, says, "People generally understand if they have to wait a few extra minutes for their food because it's my turn to sing." Still, all that rushing around can be dangerous: he once poured prime-rib juice down a lady's back.

A student's serving ability, though, has little to do with getting hired. Trudie selects her servers on the basis of their voices. She figures the rest will come with training.

As a result, she aims for CCM's best and usually gets them. Word of mouth handles the recruiting; she handles auditions in front of live audiences. The initial draw is the good money the students earn.

Yet if money is what draws employees to Forest View, something more intangible is what holds them. As trite as it sounds, the Forest View staff and owners are one big happy family: In between opera jobs, former employees regularly come to town to visit the Seybolds. Ex-servers living around the country and overseas say they keep in touch with each other to share news of the Forest View gang. All year long, the Seybolds receive long-distance phone calls (and accept collect ones) from former "family" members, and overnight guests are common. Even current employees find themselves gravitating back to work on their days off just to "hang out," testifies Maria Ventura, CCM '76.

"Trudie and Kurt are like father and mother to all of them," says Italo Tajo, former CCM professor and famed bass-baritone. "They treat them like their own sons and daughters. They are very generous people. You cannot help but love this couple."

Treating employees like "family" includes encouraging their endeavors, coaching their voices, helping them apply for scholarships, and letting them know when it is

time to move on. "They want us to leave as soon as we can," Zeller explains. "That means we are successful."

And just like a mother, Trudie loves to boast about her children who have achieved musical acclaim. On one typical Thursday, she is thrilled at her reunion with Tom Hammons, CCM '74, who recently played Kissinger in the world premiere of *Nixon in China*; Bard Suverkrop, CCM '74, MM '78; and his wife, Jan, CCM '77, who both perform with the Dusseldorf Opera in Germany. Trudie hangs portraits of all those with notable careers in the lobby's "hall of fame."

Most of those hall-of-famers would attribute a portion of their success to Forest View. Hammons, for example, points out that working at Forest View in the late '70s taught him to "communicate" with an audience. "I learned what it takes to please an audience. You have to perform to learn that."

"It's a wonderful training ground," adds Bard Suverkrop, one of Hammons' former coworkers. "Every evening you have to get up there and perform, with the smoke and the noise—all while running around serving sauerbraten. In

Above from left to right: Kirby Traylor and Alison Acord sing a medley of Irving Berlin tunes. Two guests sing along and ham it up with their waitress.

Opposite page from left to right: Used to taking care of famous diners, Richard Zeller waits on opera star Italo Tajo and Maria Marsan. A typical Thursday night fills the restaurant's long tables to capacity

Germany, I'm surprised when I hear people complain about singing in bad weather or certain air. Forest View helped me rise above that.

"Forest View is a very important part in the life of the singers at UC. At school, you get a little (stage) training here and there, but not every night like you get here."

Maria Ventura likes the variety of music she gets to sing at the restaurant—"repertoire you wouldn't normally do"—so much, in fact, that she works there temporarily between engagements with operas as far away as Florida and Germany. "It keeps you fresh," she says. "Also it looks good on a resume. The New York City Opera is impressed with Forest View repertoire."

Trudie points out one more benefit her employees gain under her tutelage—a pleasant self-assuredness. "People who are shy and timid develop a real personality. And people who are pompous come down a peg or two." Luctrician Booth agrees. "I was one of the shiest people on the face of the earth. In three years, I am ready to handle anything. Forest View forces you to come out of yourself and do what you do best—sing."

Mothering employees is only one of the things Trudie does well; the other is tending to business. Like any parent, she can be both loving and strict. When it comes to business, she insists that every detail be conducted to her standards—the right standards.

That means she takes an active role in making sure customers have a wonderful time: learning people's names and using them, publicly recognizing special guests and out-of-towners, celebrating every guest's birthday and anniversary with the whole crowd, and keeping a keen eye on everything.

Of course, part of the atmosphere is the German decor and food. Trudie entrusts the latter to her adopted son, Luciano, an opera singer in his own right who joined her as chef in 1977, but she spends time in the kitchen, too.

At present, she is particularly proud of the decor, following last year's major renovation that enlarged the main dining room and stage, created a second, smaller dining room, increased the kitchen's capabilities, improved the outdoor biergarten, and added authentic Bavarian touches like hand-painted murals of Germany and ceiling

lattice work. "We went all the way," she says with a broad grin, "and we're mortgaged to the hilt."

She frequently uses the word "we," making sure no one thinks this is a job for one woman. Her husband, Kurt, whom she married in 1983, handles most business details and takes the stage as master of ceremonies at evening performances. The two established the Klose-Seybold Opera Scholarship at CCM in 1986 in memory of their parents.

Dean Laster says their work has helped UC in several ways. One, it gives "CCM a good name" around the country. Two, it has helped approximately 250 aspiring young singers earn money for auditions, coaching, and scores. Three, it gives students "an opportunity, in a professional environment to work under pressure and have fun performing."

Since first meeting Trudie in 1976, Laster says he's grown to admire her greatly. He describes her most succinctly: "Driving, loving, talented, caring, demanding, and one smart cookie."

Many of Our Supportive Customers

Where do I begin? We had so many supportive customers. Large company groups such as the retirees of GE, Bunny Szecskay, Cincinnati Incorporated with Ed Bosse, monthly visits from our good customers such as the Melson's, Weinstein's, Mt. St. Joseph; then we had a celebration of the 1000th visit of Bruce Fields on November 3, 2000. There were the Focke's, Kriegelstein, the Bahrani's, the Bollands, Patricia Corbett and friends, the Coursey's, the Day's, the Dickinson's, the Ericson's, Eschenlohr, Feigelson, Finch, Fischesser, Frost, Gault, Gibbons, Giglio, Dr. Heidt, Wellington Orthopedic office, Hoffman, Johnson, Kane (Bill and Patty were married in our garden) Andrew White (professor of voice), Jeffrey's, Klein, Bill Myers, Betty Lehr, Jock and Pants Laurence, Dr Leon Lichtin, Sue Linden, Gus Linder, Herman Luckner, Jack Louiso, John Marcum, Mario Marsan, Jack Ward. Ed Bosse (Cincinnati Corp) Chandra Shaw, and many more. If I miss a few, remember I'm 87!

Good Food ◆ Good Drink ◆ Good Times

Forest View Gardens

10th Anniversary
Singers' Reunion

August 12, 1986

Gala program cover from Forest View Gardens

PROGRAM

RECEPTION
in Bier Garten
Cocktails and Hors D'oeuvres

DINNER
Forest View Gardens
MENU
Broiled Veal Chop Rosemary
Salmon Steak with Lemon Caper Sauce
Baked Potato
Glazed Baby Carrots
Salad   Rolls   Butter
Double Chocolate Mousse with Raspberry Glaze

TRIBUTE
to Jennie and Karl Klose
by Rev. Herman J. Helfrich

INTRODUCTIONS
by Trudie and Kurt Seybold

Maestro Italo Tajo

Patricia Corbett

Hal Laster

MUSICAL SELECTIONS
presented by FVG Alumni

"The Student Prince"
Current FVG Company

CONCLUSION
Sextet from "Lucia" — Donizetti

The Triumphal March from "Aida" — Verdi

by FVG Ensemble and Chorus

Flowers arranged by Stuart Woolley
Dorl & Fern Florist

Trudie and Kurt Seybold

History

Forest View Gardens has a rich, charming history. In the 1920s, it was called Philippe's Place. It closed in 1938 and in 1940 was reopened by Jennie Klose and named Forest View Gardens.

Jennie, a native of Bavaria, and her husband, Karl, from the Rhineland near Kaiserlautern, lived in the house on North Bend Road at the front of the property.

In 1975 the Kloses retired and offered the business to their daughter, Trudie Russell. An accomplished musician, Trudie taught choral music and coached opera for 25 years. She is a graduate of the University of Cincinnati College-Conservatory of Music and holds a double degree in Music Education and Voice, and a Master's of Education from Temple University.

Trudie remodeled Forest View Gardens into a Bavarian restuarant and introduced a new concept in restuarant entertainment. Through the assistance and encouragement of Hal Laster, Assitant Dean of Admissions at CCM, they conceived the idea of presenting excerpts from Broadway shows and hiring opera and musical theatre graduate students as singers.

Launching the idea, Trudie called on the services of Louise and Maurice Mandell, fellow graduates of CCM. They appeared as guest artists in the first musical production at Forest View Gardens — "Fiddler on the Roof."

That first production brought fame and acclaim to Forest View Gardens, and was followed by more: "Cabaret," "The Student Prince," "The King and I," etc.

As the concept developed, special credit goes to singer-pianist-composer Doug Pennington for his many arrangements, especially "Broadway Medley," "The Student Prince," "Hot on Cole," "Classical Medley," "Fiddler on the Roof."

Trudie was joined by Kurt Seybold in 1980 and since then Forest View Gardens has been a team operation. Kurt is master of ceremonies and vocalist, as well as manager of the business operation with Trudie.

Many other talented musicians have contributed to the success of Forest View Gardens. Accordianist Jack Frost and percussionist Teddy Babst, who joined us at the beginning, provide the accompaniment for the singers.

It is most rewarding for us to see our singers go on to New York and other cities here and abroad, secure in the knowledge that, in our own way, we were able to contribute to their success.

Over the years we have followed their careers. We are pleased that wherever they go, a sense of camaraderie exists among the Forest View Gardens alumni.

The lasting friendships and shared experiences have created a sense of family among our singers. Wherever they go — East, West or to Europe — they find each other and help each other. This love affair among the FVG singers is our legacy — the human element that is ever present in the way we manage the business of Forest View Gardens.

Sincerely,

Trudie & Kurt Seybold

Trudie & Kurt Seybold

Scholarship Evenings

As I mentioned earlier, Kurt established a scholarship with the UC Foundation for CCM. Our first scholarship was about $1,500, and then $5,000; now it is $10,000. The auditions are held at CCM with judges from various opera companies. According to the UC Foundation report received November 1, 2016, it totals $185,400.41. Other scholarships are offered, such as the Corbett, Alexander, Dieterle and more.

In order to contribute to the scholarship fund, we held an Opera Gala evening at Forest View Gardens. The evening would begin in the Bier Garden with appetizers and drinks. We then moved into the dining room for dinner and entertainment. These Galas were memorable occasions. Our first Gala was in 1986; the second Gala in 1989 featured Cesar-Antonio Suarez, a tenor originally from Cuba and a voice student of mine while he was at Coral Park Senior High, Miami, Florida. Mr. Suarez won international recognition after winning the coveted Giuseppe Verdi Prize. He debuted opposite Dame Joan Sutherland and Beverly Sills, and in 1989, he sang the role of Pollione in *Norma* with Dame Joan Sutherland. Kurt and I travelled to hear her farewell concert and my wonderful tenor prodigy at the Michigan Opera Theater in Detroit.

Winners of the Seybold/Russell Scholarship

1987 Eric Ashcraft, tenor, Professor at Luther University

1988 Lynda Keith McKnight, soprano, made her New York Met debut in the *Ghosts of Versailles*. She has given multitude recitals in the states and Europe. She received her MM and Artist Diploma in opera from the University of Cincinnati College of Music, and MM in vocal performance from Baylor. She lives in Texas.

1989 Lisa Erickson, soprano

1990 Dianna Heldman, mezzo-soprano

1990 Richard Teaster, pianist and tenor

1991 Donald Davis (no voice record)

1992 Robert Lomax, tenor

1993 Craig Priebe, baritone

1994 Kate Healy, soprano

1995 Sandra Kennard, soprano

1996 Teresa Dody, soprano

1997 Michelle Cooper (Giangiacomo), soprano

1998 Daniel Weeks, tenor, professor of voice at CCM

1999 Martha Guth, soprano

2001 Megan Monaghan, soprano

2002 Audrey Luna, soprano

2003 Deborah Selig, soprano (keeps in touch – Thank you, Deborah!)

2004 Elizabeth Andrews Roberts, soprano

2005 Caitlyn Lynch, soprano

2006 Bronwen Forbay, soprano

2007 Damien Pass, baritone

2008 Catherine Martin, mezzo-soprano

2009 Michael Young, baritone

2010 Deborah Nansteel, mezzo-soprano

2011 Chabrelle Williams, soprano

2012 Edward Nelson, baritone

2013 Talya Lieberman, soprano (always keeps in touch – Thank you, Talya!)

2014 Alec Carlson, tenor

2015 Christian Pursell, baritone, semi-finalist at the New York Metropolitan Opera National Council

2016 Murrella Parton, soprano, who also won the Three Arts Competition of which I was one of judges

---

I attended the District Met auditions on November 7, 2016, at CCM. Two of the judges used to wait tables at FVG: Kelly Anderson, who is Executive Director of Grand Junction Symphony Orchestra in Colorado, and Thomas Bankston, Artistic Director of the Dayton Opera Company.

Being on the Board, I was simply enjoying all the singers. To my surprise, our 2015 scholarship winner sang a marvelous competition. I was not surprised that Christian Pursell, baritone, was selected to sing at the next level of the competition, the Regional in Chicago, and was a semi-finalist of the New York Metropolitan Opera Company.

On April 19, 2016 we featured the last three winners at Evergreen Retirement Community for the residents' enjoyment.

Management

Our first manager was my son Eddie, who did a great job, but his heart and soul were not in the restaurant business. He still loved boats and sunny Florida, so with his wife Lori and baby Nicole, they moved back to the Tampa, Florida area. Now he is the owner of his own boat business, Viage Group, in Sarasota. Eddie and Lori are proud grandparents, and of course that makes me a very proud great-grandmother. Dr. Nicole and Michael Howe had a baby boy, Quade; and Kelly and Michael Rothman, with baby girl Isa Bella. They now live sunny Florida.

We trained our very capable Tim Giglio, a graduate from Western Hills High School who started as a floor cleaner, then busser and chef, and finally manager of the business, until 1992 when he resigned and joined UBS Financial. Tim is my financial advisor and investor. Kurt and I took over the management of the restaurant then, and it was a success.

Successful Show Place

We became the show dining center of greater Cincinnati. Many of our singers have had operatic and musical successes. One of our original basses, Thomas Hammons of Cincinnati, has been with the New York Metropolitan Opera for many years and still is singing with other companies throughout our country. This summer he will sing in our *Tosca*. Helene Schneiderman sang several years with the Heidelberg Opera Company and is an artist with the Stuttgart Opera Company; she will be singing at the New York Metropolitan Opera in the *Rosenkavalier* in 2017. Lisa Griffith has been singing with the Deutsche Oper am Rhein, and we were fortunate to hear her several years ago at the Dortmont Opera as Sophie in the *Rosenkavlier*. Magnificent production! We saw Sue Benkin at the Hamburg Theater Germany singing in *Cats*, and while in Germany, we met our pianist and arranger Scott Lawton, who was directing *Miss Saigon* and who also arranged the *Miss Saigon* for us.

Romantic Dream Vocations

Kurt and I had traveled to the most beautiful vacation spots in the world. Both of us had worked very hard all our lives, and now FVG gave us two to three weeks in January to venture to the magnificent, warm, sunny Caribbean Islands; Italy; Austria; Germany; and a few wonderful excursions to New York City. Our favorite island was St. John's, one of the three American Virgin Islands. We stayed at the magnificent Caneel Bay. We even owned some property above Cruz Bay, but it was difficult to reach this mountain property, so we sold it. We planned my seventieth birthday at a private estate with our friends Bill and Patty Kane in November of 1999. Bill and Patty brought several cases of wine, and Kurt and I brought veal chops. All of a sudden, we heard the news broadcast telling us that a hurricane was hitting Puerto Rico and traveling in our direction. Hurricanes were never expected that late in the year. We were advised to leave the property immediately, which we did, and were escorted to St. Thomas. We found some reservations at the Ritz Carlton with no electric, and boxed breakfast, lunch, and dinners. We finally flew out of St. Thomas back to the States unharmed. Kurt's gift to me was his giving up smoking cigarettes, a habit since he was fifteen.

We also took quite a few Caribbean cruises with the Princess and Norwegian ships, twice through the Panama Canal, and once with Eddie and Jay. We had a delightful cruise to the Panama with Mathias and Gertrude Haugh, Kurt's dearest friends from Memmingen, Germany. We loved Cancun and Punta Cana in the Dominica Republic. The bartender at Punta Cana remembered us three years in a row. When we arrived and he saw Kurt, he would shout, "Here comes Pappa Kurt, and here is your CC Manhattan." Yes, Kurt loved his Manhattans. On his fiftieth birthday, I had planned a surprise party on the Mike Fink River boat with cousins from Germany, the Tajo's, and many wonderful guests. Rosie Melzer brought him a shirt. He loved, in order, America, CC Manhattans, and Trudie. Ben and Shirley Bernstein made the party a success.

We traveled to Hawaii and stayed in Maui and the Big Island. Many of my fellow students who had graduated with me from CCM were still living there, and we had fun visiting them. We made a trip to Germany with my son Jay after his organ transplant because he wanted to meet his heritage. We also spent some time in Italy and attended *Aida* in the outdoor Arena in Verona.

One year, we visited the Bottenbergs in Montreal, and another time, the FVG singers performed in Canada and then visited Niagara Falls. We loved our Island hopping:

Grand Cayman, Aruba, St. Croix, Jamaica, Nevis, St.John, St.Thomas, Punta Cana in the Dominican Republic. We took several cruises, even one with Inelda Tajo.

J. B. Russell IV and Edward Allen Russell (L to R)

My Family

Eddie and Lori live in Odessa, Florida; they had two girls: Kelly, married to Michael Rothman; and Dr. Nicole, married to Michael Howe. Kelly has one daughter Bella, and Nicole has a little boy, Quade. Jay passed away in 2003 after having a pancreas and kidney transplant in 1994. It was successful; he lived nine good years. I was a volunteer for the Juvenile Diabetes Foundation. We attended a Diabetes Gala at the Music Hall presented by the Clooney family. Attending were George, Rosie, Nic, and his wife.

Jay's wife Susie lives in Palm Beach County. Jay and Susie had a beautiful girl, Lacy, who is a cardio nurse, and twin sons. Christopher is an artistic iron worker with two precious children: Jillian, 10 going on 30, and Christopher Bryan; and Jason is an artistic tile and floor setter and a professional surfer.

The Final Curtain

It was very difficult to close the infamous Forest View Gardens, but no one wanted to resume the concept. It was time to retire. On June 1, 2001, with a packed seating, Kurt sang "Auf Weidersehn" for the last time.

The College Conservatory was well represented that evening. Patty Corbett sat at the front, Stamm Tisch and Louise Nippert sat in the rear with the Dean and friends. Kurt sang his favorite Sinatra song, and instead of singing "My Way," he invited me on the stage and sang "Our Way." We didn't cry, but we were relieved of the pressure.

Kurt suffered heart problems, stenosis of the aorta, and needed a heart valve. I had read about a method performed at the Cleveland Clinic. We heard that the same procedure was done at Christ Hospital here in Cincinnati. But the operation was not a success, and he passed away at Wellspring, with me by his side, and at only 76 years of age on April 7, 2014.

In 2011 we had moved to Evergreen Retirement Community located near Wyoming in Hartwell. We were in the Assisted Living Complex and had a charming apartment with room for the Steinway and a few antiques. Lacy and

Christopher flew to Cincy from Florida, rented a U-Haul truck, and took some of the precious heirlooms back to Florida. Lacy loves antiques and Christopher loved all the iron art work that my father had made.

So this brings my memories to a close I am surviving, but lonely. I miss my Boopie. Luciano cares for me, stays with me a few days each week, and has given recitals here at Evergreen. I also have a furry kitten named Annette. I have been blessed, and I will continue to enjoy my life.

As if all those blessings weren't enough, I have been awarded a number of honors:

On April 15, 1988, I received the alumnae award from UC College Conservatory of Music. It was presented to me by Dean Robert J. Werner and Paul Hillner, President of the Alumnae Association.

I became an honorary member of the Cincinnati Opera Board and received my 50th anniversary diploma from my professional music fraternity, Sigma Alpha Iota, International Music Fraternity.

To my surprise, on April 30, 2016, I was awarded the Western Hills High School Maroon Award for exceptional achievement in the community. My son Eddie enjoyed this special occasion.

CCM DISTINGUISHED ALUMNI AWARD

Gertrude Klose Seybold (Certificate in voice '51, CCM: B.S. '51, music education, UC) is a Cincinnati-born alumna of the University of Cincinnati College-Conservatory of Music who went on to make her mark as a performer and teacher in Norfolk, Va., and its Tidewater area; in southeastern Florida; in Philadelphia, Pa. Now, as an established restaurateur in Cincinnati, she continues to help aspiring young singers achieve their career goals.

In Virginia for two years after her CCM graduation, Gertrude Klose was in demand as a singer-recitalist and recognized by the State Board of Education as one of the most creative music teachers in the system.

In Florida, 1953-68, she served as choral director for the Dade County School System in Miami, where she also coached and taught voice, and was choral clinician and judge for high school choral festivals. For her teaching of Latin-speaking scholarship students, many of whom now sing professionally in the United States and Europe, she won special acclaim. Active, too, in the Dade County Opera Company, Klose established its first opera programs for the public schools. In addition, she was president of Sigma Alpha Iota Alumnae Professional Music Sorority and president of the Coral Gables and Miami Federated Music Clubs of America. She served eight years as minister of music at Sunset Presbyterian Church, directing ten choirs, in the Gables.

After moving to Philadelphia in 1968, Gertrude Klose resumed teaching choral music and became assistant choral director of the Philadelphia All-City Choirs. She also wrote a one-year music curriculum for an alternative school program and received a master's degree in music education from Temple University in 1974.

A year later, she returned to Cincinnati to take over her parents' restaurant, Forest View Gardens, and conceived the idea of combining the restaurant's old-world German atmosphere with fine music. To date, some 250 aspiring young opera singers from CCM have had the opportunity to work and sing at Forest View Gardens, polishing their craft and earning extra money for coaching, auditions, and scores.

In 1986, Gertrude Klose Seybold and her husband, Kurt, established the Klose-Seybold Opera Scholarship at CCM in memory of their parents. Last April the first scholarship went to CCM graduate student R. Eric Ashcraft.

On behalf of all who have benefited from the talent, generosity and hospitality of Gertrude Klose Seybold and her husband, Kurt, we present this CCM Distinguished Alumni Award with our sincere thanks and good wishes.

April 15, 1988

Paul R. Hillner
President
CCM Alumni Association

Robert J. Werner
CCM Dean

Thomas James Kelly
Professor of Music

Trudie's CCM Distinguished Alumni Award.

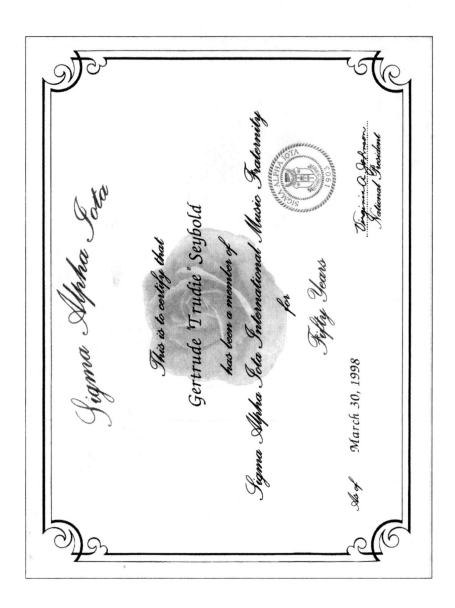

UNIVERSITY OF CINCINNATI

THE UNIVERSITY OF CINCINNATI AND ITS ALUMNI ASSOCIATION
ARE PROUD TO PRESENT TO

GERTRUDE SEYBOLD

THIS TESTIMONIAL
TO MARK WITH CONGRATULATIONS AND
WELL-WISHING
YOUR INDUCTION AS A MEMBER OF

THE GOLDEN BEARCAT CLUB

HONORING YOUR ROLE IN ESTABLISHING
THE UNIVERSITY'S RICH HERITAGE AND TRADITIONS

June 10, 2001

President
University of Cincinnati

President
Alumni Association

Evergreen Retirement Community's promotional flyer highlighting Trudie's Oktoberfest recipes. Also used in the Cincinnati Enquirer.

RECIPES FROM

Forest View Gardens

ariaffair

PROGRAM
August 30, 1989

An Evening of Music and Feasting
to benefit the Klose-Seybold Memorial Scholarship Fund
at the University of Cincinnati College-Conservatory of Music

Forest View Gardens

Established in 1939 by Karl and Jennie Klose

50th ANNIVERSARY YEAR!

Famous Recipes

To conclude my memoir, I want to include some of our secret recipes. My mother's famous potato balls are a winner, and I am sure that you will enjoy making them. Mama Jennie would not give our customers a clue how to make them. Some of scientific customers took them home and placed them under a microscope. Our schnitzel recipes were either created by my mother or me. When Kurt and I traveled to various Austrian or German villages, we managed to detect the ingredients of various dishes. So I am happy to now share some of the most popular and delicious recipes. I have included recipes of our beloved friends and customers.

Cookbook illustrations from the original AriaAffair Cookbook by Teddy Babst.

Recipes

Forest View's Chicken Liver Pâté

2 lbs. of chicken livers

1 clove garlic, minced

1/4 c. olive oil or chicken fat

1 t. basil

Bunch of fresh parsley

1 t. marjoram

1 med. chopped onion

Salt and white pepper to taste

Clean and devein chicken livers. Heat oil in a heavy skillet. Saute all ingredients until livers are done and onions are transparent, not burned. Place mixture into food processor and with blade, puree into pate. Refrigerate and serve with a good German or Jewish rye bread.

Mama Klose

Emmenthaler Gebacken

6 slices of a solid swiss or emmenthaler cheese, cut by your deli - 1/2" thick, 4x4 cut into triangles.

1/2 c. milk

Flour

Bread crumbs

1 egg

Fry daddy or heavy skillet with 3" of hot oil or crisco

Blanch each slice of cheese with flour. Dip into egg wash, and roll in bread crumbs. Heat oil, 450 degrees and fry cheese until golden brown. Serve immediately.

Variations:

Forest View Onion Rings

Cut approximately 3 large Bermuda onions in slices. Rinse in ice cool water. Drain and pat dry and follow directions above.

Forest View Eggplant

Cut 1 large peeled eggplant into 1/2" strips. Soak eggplant in hot salt water solution to remove bitter taste. Drain and pat dry. Follow above directions. Serve with cocktail sauce.

Forest View Zucchini Strips

Take 6 medium size zucchini and cut into strips 1/2" wide. Follow above directions. Serve with cocktail sauce.

Trudie Seybold

Forest View Gardens Sauerkraut Balls

6 ozs. hot pork sausage	1 lb. sauerkraut
3 ozs. cream cheese	2 T. bread crumbs
1 sm. minced onion	Pepper to taste
2 minced garlic cloves	1 egg (slightly beaten)
1/4 c. chopped parsley	1/2 c. water

Saute pork sausage in heavy skillet. Add onion, garlic, parsley and saute until completely done. Set aside. Drain and wash sauerkraut, if it is extremely salty. In mixing bowl, add sauerkraut with sausage mixture.

Thoroughly mix cheese and add bread crumbs. Add enough bread crumbs so it easily forms a ball the size of a ping pong ball. Beat egg with water. Dip each ball in egg wash and drain. Roll in bread crumbs. These can be made a day before serving.

Heat grease until very hot, drop balls into deep fry until dark brown, or until balls float to the top. Serve immediately.

Mama Klose's German Sweet & Sour Dressing

1 c. oil

1/4 c. cider vinegar

3 cloves of garlic, diced

1/2 c. water

Sugar, salt and white pepper to taste

For Italian variation, add 1 t. of fresh crushed basil and oregano.

Mix and store in air tight container.

Jennie Klose

Forest View's Maurice Dressing

When preparing our house salad, we mix the salad greens with the above dressing and add:

Creamy Maurice Dressing:

2 c. German Sweet and Sour Dressing

1 1/2 c. mayonnaise

1 c. sour cream

Mix together

If dressing is too thin, add more mayonnaise. Taste and add salt or sugar to taste.

Top salad with a ladle of Maurice, sliced onion, grated onions, sliced mushrooms, tomatoes and crispy fried bacon.

Trudie Seybold

Mama Klose's German Potato Salad

5 lbs. red bliss potatoes

1/4 c. chopped parsley

1 sm. onion chopped

3/4 c. chopped celery

1/4 c. chopped scallions or chives

1/2 c. chicken stock or bouillon

Cider vinegar, oil, salt, white pepper and sugar to taste

Serve room temperature, NOT HOT!!

Variation:

Add: 1/2 c. crumbled fried bacon and reserve 1/2 c. hot grease. Eliminate oil.

Mama Klose

Chicken Marsala

1 1/2 lbs. chicken breast (boneless)*

1/4 stick butter or margarine

1/4 c. of flour for blanching

2 cloves of minced garlic

2 c. mushrooms, either plain or shitake

Soup stock or beef bouillon

1/2 c. of sweet Marsala wine (optional)

Minced parsley for garnish

Melt butter in heavy skillet. When frothy, add blanched chicken breast pieces, burn lightly on both sides. Add garlic, mushrooms and stock. Let simmer for approx. 5 min. Add wine and ignite. Simmer to reduce broth. Add salt and pepper to taste. Serve immediately. Garnish with minced parsley. Serve with Spatzle. Serves 4 people

*Veal cutlets may be substituted for chicken.

Trudie Seybold

Chicken Rosemary

4 boneless, skinless chicken breasts

1 T. clarified butter (low sat. oil)

1/4 c. heavy cream

1/2 t. ground rosemary

Salt and white pepper to taste

Take chicken breasts, place between two pieces of wax paper, and pound with tenderizer mallet until very thin.

Heat clarified butter in heavy cast iron skillet. Blanch both sides of chicken breasts with flour and place in hot butter. Be careful not to burn them. Remove breasts when light golden brown on both sides. Place on serving platter.

Place skillet on burner and slowly add 1/4 c. heavy cream into chicken drippings. Stir until smooth and thick. Add salt and white pepper to taste. Add 1/2 t. rosemary.

Return chicken to skillet and cook 5 min. Remove breasts and gravy to platter and garnish with fresh sprigs of rosemary. This dish is delicious with either buttered noodles, home-made German Spatzle or rice.

Trudie Seybold

Wiener Schnitzel

4 pes. of veal cutlets, fat trimmed and pounded

1 egg

1/4 c. milk

1 c. corn flake crumbs

1/2 c. wesson oil

Whisk egg and milk. Dip veal into egg wash and then crumbs. Heat oil in large skillet, do not burn oil, and fry on each side until golden brown. Serve with lemon wedge and chopped parsley. Serves 4.

Zigeuner Schnitzel

6 pes. veal cutlets, pounded   Bread crumbs

1 egg   1/2 c. oil or crisco

1/4 c. milk

Blanch each piece of veal and dip into egg wash. Coat each side with bread crumbs. Refrigerate until topping is prepared.

Topping:

1 lrg. Red pepper   1 lrg. tomato

1 lrg. Green pepper   2 T. butter

1 lrg. Onion   2 cloves minced garlic

1 c. white mushrooms   1 c. Burgundy wine

Saute butter and garlic. Cut vegetables into approx. 1/8" wide strips. Sauté the vegetables until nice and crispy, not soggy. Add mushrooms at the very end with the tomato. Add wine, salt and pepper to taste. Keep this mixture warm.

Heat oil in heavy skillet and fry schnitzels on each side until golden brown. Pour vegetable mixture on top and serve immediately. (Serves 6).

Trudie Seybold

Sauerbraten

Marinade:

2 c. water

1 c. chablis

1 lrg. diced onion

2 peeled garlic cloves

5 black whole peppercorns

4 whole juniper berries

2 small bay leaves

2 stalks of diced celery

1/2 c. cubed carrots

Small bunch parsley

6 lbs. boneless beef roast, preferably top or bottom round or rump

3 T. butter

2 lrg. garlic cloves

1/2 c. diced carrots

1/2 c. diced onions

2 T. flour

1/2 c. water

1 T. au jus base

2 T. sour cream

In a 2-3 qt. saucepan, combine the wine, water, vinegar, onion garlic, crushed peppercorns, juniper berries, bay leaves, celery and parsley. Bring marinade to a boil and let simmer for 10 minutes. Remove from heat and cool to room temperature. Place beef into a deep crock and pour marinade. Refrigerate for several days. The longer marinated the better the flavor. Remove meat from marinade and strain liquid. RESERVE LIQUID. Pat dry the meat. In a large iron roaster, melt butter and brown meat on both sides. Add vegetables and brown together with au jus. Remove meat and stir in flour to make a browned roux. Add water and taste for desired thickness. Add 2 c. of reserve marinade. Boil gravy and add more flour roux if too thin. Return meat to the casserole. Cover tightly and simmer over low heat for 2 hours or until done. Transfer meat to heated platter. Add sour cream to gravy, salt and pepper to taste.

If you wish, add more sour cream and more chablis. Skim any fat off the top. Cut meat into 1/4" slices and arrange on heated platter. Ladle gravy over the top and sprinkle with fresh chopped parsley. Serve with dumplings.

Mama Klose

Mama Klose's Famous Potato Balls

6 lrg. Idaho potatoes

1 tsp. salt

1/4 lb. margarine or butter

4 egg yolks

1/2 c. Wisconsin spread cheddar cheese

3/4 c. flour

Salt to taste

Cut potatoes into quarters and cover with hot water. Add salt and bring to a boil. Let boil uncovered until potatoes are tender not MUSHY. Drain all excess water and return to low flame and dry potatoes. THIS IS THE SECRET.

Place potatoes in electric mixing bowl. Do not use FOOD PROCESSOR. Use the whip, and slowly whip potatoes. Add 1/4 lb. margarine or butter, 4 egg yolks, no whites, 1/2 c. Wisconsin spread Cheddar cheese. Slowly fold in approximately 3/4 cup flour. Salt to taste. Roll into miniature balls, (size of a ping pong ball) and roll in bread crumbs. These can be made ahead of time and stored in refrigerator. Do not freeze.

Deep fry in heavy 2 qt. sauce pan, or Fry Daddy, until golden brown and floating to the top. (Serves 8 people).

Mama Klose's Secret Potato Ball recipes. Good Luck! I never measure Mama Klose's recipes.

Forest View's Potato Pancakes

6 med. potatoes, peeled	1 T. minced parsley
2 T. flour	1/4 t. baking powder
1 1/2 t. salt	2 eggs, well beaten
1/2 c. minced onion	Oil or crisco (1/4" deep)

Combine flour, salt and baking powder. Set aside. Wash, pare and finely grate potatoes. Set aside. Heat fat in a heavy skillet, over low heat. Combine the flour mixture with eggs, onion and parsley. Drain liquid that collects from grated potatoes. Add potatoes to egg mixture and beat thoroughly with spoon. When fat is hot, spoon about 2 T. batter for each pancake into fat, leaving about 1" between pancakes. Cook over medium heat until golden brown and crisp on one side. Turn carefully and brown other side. Drain on paper towel. Serve with Sauerbraten or with sour cream and applesauce.

Makes about 20 medium size pancakes.

Variation: 1 1/2 t. caraway seeds.

Trudie Seybold

Kraut Krapfen
(Sauerkraut Dumplings)

Noodle dough:

1 lb. flour	1/4 t. caraway seed
2 eggs	Pepper to taste
Some water	1/2 c. margarine
1 lb. sauerkraut	1/2 c. Soup stock
1/2 c. Diced ham	

Make your noodle dough. On noodle board, roll out dough and make a large thin sheet. Let dough rest for about 10 min. Use cooked sauerkraut which has been seasoned with caraway seeds, ham and drain thoroughly. Spread mixture on noodle dough and roll (as a jelly roll), cut roll into 2" slices. Heat margarine in a large iron kettle and place dumplings side by side and gently brown on each side. Add soup stock and slowly steam dumplings.

Serve with a salad. Serves 4

Spätzle
(Small Bavarian Dumplings)

2 qts. water	1 stick butter
4 eggs	1 t. salt
3 c. all-purpose flour	

In large mixing bowl combine the flour, 1/2 t. salt, add lightly beaten eggs and milk. The dough must be very thick. Bring 2 qts. water and 1/2 t. salt to boil. Use a Spatzle machine or a colander with large holes. Pour batter into machine or colander and add batter to boiling water. When dumplings rise to the surface, take a strainer and gather them and rinse off with cold water. Before serving, melt butter in a heavy iron skillet. Add dumplings and brown lightly. Turn only once and place on a hot platter. Garnish with parsley.

Apple Strudel

3 lbs. sliced and peeled apples

1/2 c. sugar

1/2 c. brown sugar

2 t. cinnamon

1/2 c. raisins

1/2 c. melted butter

1 pkg. puff pastry

Unroll puff pastry and follow directions on package. Mix apples with sugar, cinnamon and raisins. Brush dough with butter and place apples in center. Overlap and brush with butter. Bake in 400 degree oven until light brown or crust puffy.

Trudie Seybold

Forest View Garden's Kaiser Pudding

1 qt. milk

2 c. fine dry bread crumbs, stale bread or roll

4 egg yolks

4 egg whites, stiffly beaten

1/2 c. sugar

1/2 c. butter

2 t. vanilla

2 T. powdered sugar

Cream butter with sugar and eggs. Pour milk over bread crumbs. Combine these two mixtures and add vanilla. Pour in shallow buttered baking dish and bake in moderate oven, 325 degrees, until set. Take out of oven and spread strawberry preserves over the top. To make *meringue, whip the four egg whites and add two T. powdered sugar. Spread over the top to make a light meringue. Return to mod. oven and cook until the meringue is set and light brown.

*We make a variation of this recipe. Instead of using meringue and preserves, add 1-6 oz. pkg. of chocolate chips or 1 c. of crushed pineapple, 1 1/2 c. tart red cherries or 3/4 c. of raisins and chopped walnuts.

Trudie's Collectibles

Chocolate Mousse Cake

1 lb. semi-sweet chocolate	6 T. powdered sugar
2 c. heavy whipping cream	Chocolate cookie crumbs
6 eggs	9" Spring Form Pan

In a double-boiler, melt chocolate. Separate 4 eggs. Beat 4 egg yolks and 2 whole eggs until lemon color. Whip egg whites until stiff. Also whip heavy cream and fold into powdered sugar. After chocolate has cooled slightly, pour into egg yolk mixture. Fold in stiffly beaten whites and whipping cream. Take a 9" spring form pan and coat the bottom of the pan with pam and chocolate cookie crumbs. Pour mousse into form and chill until set.

Cut and serve immediately. Top with whipping cream.

Laura Nestor, Wyncote, PA

Hungarian Finger Torte

5 c. flour	1 lb. margarine or butter
3 pkgs. yeast	4 eggs
1/4 c. sugar	1 1/2 c. sugar
1 c. lukewarm water	1 t. salt
2 c. milk	

Put flour in a large bowl. Make a well. Add yeast and sugar. Pour in lukewarm water. Stir and make a little batter. Scald milk and add margarine or butter. Cool. Beat eggs, add sugar and salt. Add to cooled milk mixture. Slowly stir into flour and yeast mixture. The secret is to beat the dough thoroughly and hard - until the dough gets air bubbles. Cover dough with a towel and let it rise until doubled.

Filling:

1 box brown sugar	1/2 c. granulated sugar
1 c. grated walnuts	3/4 lb. margarine or butter (melted)
2 tsp. cinnamon	

Mix together brown sugar, walnuts, cinnamon and sugar. Grease an angel food pan. When dough has risen, take a small amount and make balls, dropping them into the melted butter and then into the brown sugar mixture. Then drop into greased tube pan, one on top of the other. Do not place balls any higher than 1/2 the pan. Cover and let rise again to top.

Place in preheated 350 degrees oven. Bake until golden brown. Top with confectionary glaze-water and confectionary glaze sugar.

Trudie Seybold

Pumpkin Cheesecake

1 1/2 lbs. cream cheese	1 t. ground cloves
1 c. granulated sugar	1 t. ground ginger
4 lrg. eggs, lightly beaten	1 c. heavy cream
3 egg yolks, lightly beaten	1 T. vanilla
3 T. all-purpose flour	1 lb. can pumpkin (mashed)
2 t. ground cinnamon	

Preheat oven to 425 degrees.

In a large mixing bowl, beat together, the cream cheese, sugar, eggs and yolks. Add flour, cinnamon, cloves and ginger. Beat in the cream and vanilla. Add mashed pumpkin and beat at medium speed with electric mixer or food processor until just mixed thoroughly. Pour mixture into prepared shortbread crust 10" spring form pan and bake for 15 min. Reduce heat to 275 degrees and bake for an additional hour. Turn off the heat, BUT LEAVE THE CAKE IN THE OVEN OVERNIGHT TO COOL.

Serve cake either warm or chilled with whipped cream.

Luciano Moral, Augusta, KY

Trudie's Dutch Apple Cake
(Taught by Her Mama, Jennie)

Crust:

1 c. butter	2 1/4 sifted flour
3/4 c. sugar	1/4 t. salt
1 t. lemon rind	2 egg yolks

Cream butter. Add sugar, egg yolks, lemon rind, sifted flour and salt. This can all be done in the food processor. Chill dough. Use as needed. Can be stored for at least a week in the refrigerator. Use a 12" pie pan or oblong pan.

Filling:

6 med. apples	1/2 c. sugar
1 t. lemon rind	1 t. cinnamon

Mix above ingredients together

2 eggs (room temperature)	3/4 c. sour cream
1/4 c. sugar	3 T. butter
1/2 t. lemon rind	3/4 c. cornflake crumbs

Beat eggs until foamy. Add sugar and lemon rind until very thick and lemon color. HAND MIX sour cream into mixture. Pour over apples.

Brown cornflake crumbs and add a little sugar for taste. Sprinkle crumbs over cake.

Bake at 350 degrees until set and golden brown. If you prefer, you can prebake crust, depending how soft the apples.

Escargots Ala Trudie

(Serves 6)

Snail Butter:

1/2 lb. butter, cut in pieces	2 T. fresh parsley leaves, with stems removed
6 shallots, peeled and halved	1/2 t. salt
2 cloves of garlic	1/4 t. white pepper

Place above ingredients into food processor with blade knife. Make several rotations until all ingredients are blended. Store in refrigerator.

Snail butter 36 snails

Place a small quantity of snail butter in each snail shell. Add 1 snail to each shell, then cover with remaining butter, sealing openings. Set snails in a large, flat flameproof casserole or use the small pans specifically indented for holding snail shells, and broil until the butter is hot and bubbling. Serve immediately with delicious Italian bread.

Trudie Seybold

Trudie's Quiche Lorraine

9" ready made pastry shell or check my receipe for a flaky pastry shell

6 pieces of bacon

3/4 c. shredded swiss cheese

4 eggs, slightly beaten

2 c. heavy cream

1/4 c. chopped green onions (optional)

1 1/2 T. melted butter

1 t. red cayenne pepper

Salt and white pepper to taste

Brown bacon and crumble. Place cheese and bacon in pastry shell. Mix salt, pepper, cayenne pepper and butter into egg mixture. Strain mixture over cheese and bacon pie shell.

Bake in mod. oven, 375 degrees, for 30-35 min., until set. Serve warm. Serves 4.

Trudie Seybold

Flädla Suppe •
(Beef Consomme With Sliced German Pancakes)

1 lb. boneless lean beef cubes	Salt and pepper to taste
2 qts. cold water	1 c. coarsely diced peeled celery root
1 lrg. onion, peeled and chopped	1 c. coarsely diced leeks
1 sm. bay leaf	1/2 c. coarsely diced carrots

Place boneless lean beef in large soup pot with water. Bring beef and water to boil; reduce heat to the lowest point. Add onion, bay leaf, and vegetables; cook until meat and vegetables are tender. Strain broth and chill. Skim off any visible fat. You may want to save the meat and make cold meat salad.

Flädla (German Pancakes)

3 eggs	1/2 c. milk
3/4 c. flour	

Beat eggs, slowly. Add flour, milk and salt to taste in blender. In a large skillet, melt Crisco; pour about 1/4 c. batter into hot fat, brown on one side and flip over, then remove onto a paper towel. Continue making pancakes. They should be thin, but not as thin as crepes. When pancakes have cooled, roll each pancake and slice very thinly. Bring broth to a boil, place pancakes in soup bowl, and pour soup over pancakes. Add chives and fresh nutmeg.

Mama Klose

Home Made Chicken Soup With Farina Balls

Stock:

1 lrg. whole chicken	Enough water to cover chicken
1 onion, diced	2 lrg. carrots, diced
1 t. thyme	2 t. chicken base grandulars

Place chicken, vegetables and chicken base in a large soup kettle, and cover with water. On a high flame, let the water and chicken come to a boil. Let chicken boil briskly for 5 min., and turn flame off. Let stand in water bath for 1 hour. It will become very tender and done. Take chicken out of pot and place on a platter. Make either chicken salad or debone chicken and put meat in soup. Also good for chicken ala king. Strain broth, cool and refrigerate. After soup is cold, skim off visible fat.

Farina Balls

3 1/2 c. milk	1/4 t. fresh nutmeg, grated
1/2 t. salt	1 t. minced parsley
2/3 c. farina	1 t. chicken base
2 eggs, lightly beaten	Salt and pepper to taste
1/4 t. lemon rind, grated	2 T. butter

In a 2 qt. saucepan, bring milk to a boil. Add farina, stirring constantly on a low temperature. Add butter, parsley, chicken base and lemon rind. Remove from flame and fold in lightly, beaten eggs. Return to the stove and on low temperature stir in nutmeg, salt and pepper to taste. Cool and refrigerate.

When batter is stiff, make individual balls with a tablespoon the size of a ping pong ball. Dip your hands in cold water and form evenly shaped balls. Place balls on a platter. Take the skimmed, drained soup stock and heat. When soup comes to a boil, drop in desired amount of farina balls. Turn flame down and let simmer. When farina balls float to top, they are cooked. Ladle 3 balls per serving into a soup bowl and enjoy. Serving for 4.

Trudie Seybold

Mock Turtle Soup

3 lbs. beef

1 lb. veal

Some marrow bones

1 #2 1/2 can of tomatoes

1 bottle of catsup

1 1/2 c. diluted and sweetened vinegar

4 onions, diced

4 lrg. carrots, diced

8 hard boiled eggs

2 lemons, sliced thin

1 bunch of parsley

1 stalk of celery

8 whole cloves

8 whole allspice

6 bay leaves

1 T. mixed spices

4 c. browned flour

Worcestershire sauce to taste

Place meat and enough water to cover in a large kettle. Put all spices into a cheesecloth bag. Place flour in a heavy iron skillet over a very hot flame, brown and stir until all the flour is dark brown, but not burned. After meat is tender strain, and grind. Add eggs, carrots, catsup, vinegar, Worcestershire sauce and sliced lemons t broth. While soup is boiling, add browned flour and season to taste.

Mrs. Hoinke, Fairfield, OH

White Bean Soup

1 lrg. ham bone or 2 ham hocks

2 lbs. white dry beans

Water to cover beans

1 lb. white turnips, peeled and sliced

1 lb. potatoes, peeled and diced

1 lrg. cabbage, sliced

Bunch of collard greens, chopped

1 lrg. onion, diced

4 garlic cloves, minced

1/2 lb. pepperoni or chorizos

Salt and white pepper to taste

Soak beans overnight. In a large soup pot add beans and the above ingredients. Cover with water. Cook until tender. Stir occasionally. Be careful not to burn the soup. Add salt and pepper to taste.

Luciano Moral, Augusta, KY

Champagne Dressing

3/4 c. cider vinegar	1 t. dry mustard
2 c. crisco oil	1 t. salt
1 lrg. onion, diced	1 t. celery seed
3/4 c. sugar	

Mix all ingredients together in a blender. Makes 1 quart.

Harlene Babst, Cincinnti, OH

Russian Dressing

3 cloves minced garlic	1/2 c. sweet relish
2 c. mayonnaise	1/2 c. chives or finely cut scallions
1 c. sour cream	
1 c. chili sauce	Salt, lemon juice, white pepper and sugar to taste

Mix together and store in air tight container.

Trudie Seybold

Blue Cheese Dressing

2 c. mayonnaise	1 c. blue cheese
2 c. sour cream	1/2 c. chives
3 cloves minced garlic	Salt, white pepper and sugar to taste.
Juice from one lemon	

Mix together and store in air-tight container.

Trudie Seybold

German Meat Salad

1 lb. soup meat, left over roast or boiled tongue

1 sm. diced onion

1/4 c. oil

Vinegar, salt, pepper and sweeten to taste

Slice meat thinly, and add above ingredients. Chill overnight and serve.

Jennie Klose

Jello Salad

1 large cool whip

1 sm. lime jello (dry)

1 lb. cottage cheese

1 can fruit cocktail (drain well)

Mix cool whip and jello thoroughly. Add cottage cheese and drained fruit cocktail. Refrigerate.

Lee Witham Cincinnati, OH

Spinach Salad

1 pkg. of pre-washed fresh spinach	3 hard boiled eggs, diced
1 c. fresh bean sprouts	1/4 c. sugar
1 5 oz. can waterchestnuts	1 c. oil
1 5 oz. can bamboo shoots	1/4 c. vinegar
1/2 lb. bacon	1/3 c. catsup
1 sm. onion, chopped	1/2 t. Worcestershire sauce
	Salt and pepper to taste.

Marinate all ingredients overnight, except spinach, egg and bacon. Fry bacon until crisp and then crumble. Add to spinach and toss well before adding eggs and bacon. Serve at room temperature.

Kenneth Cytraus, Cincinnati, OH

Empinadas Fritas Spanish Meat Pies

Dough:

3 c. flour	2 T. dry sherry
1/2 t. salt	1/2 c. milk
1/2 c. lard	1/2 c. water
2 T. oil	

Combine lard, oil, sherry, milk and water. Heat in sauce pan to lukewarm temperature)

Mix above ingredients together gently. Roll out dough very thin. Work the dough as little as possible. Cut into 4" circles. Place meat filling in center using egg wash on outer rim of circle. Fold over and seal with either the prongs of a fork or a ravioli cutter.

Meat Filling:

2 lbs. lean ground beef   1 T. olive oil

Saute above in heavy skillet and add:

1 lrg. chopped onion   1 T. capers

Dash of salt and pepper   2 T. cocktail sauce or tomato puree

3/4 c. chopped green pimento olives

1/2 t. cumin

1/4 c. raisins   1 t. oregano

Deep fry in heavy sauce pan or Fry Daddy. Drain and salt to taste.

Other fillings may be used, such as strawberry jam or other jams and fill dough as above. Fry and dust with powdered sugar. Makes a delicious dessert!

Luciano Moral, Augusta, KY

Beef Brisket

3-4 lbs. brisket of beef   Season with garlic, salt and pepper

1 lrg. can tomato sauce

In foil lined pan, place seasoned Brisket and cover with tomato sauce. Seal with a cover of foil and bake in 325 degree oven for 4 hours. Slice very thin diagonally.

Lee Witham Cincinnati, OH

Teller Fleisch
(Brisket of Beef on a Plate)

4-6 lbs. lean brisket	1/2 bunch parsley
2 bay leaves	2 sliced carrots, diced
2 whole cloves	2 large onions, chopped
8 juniper berries	1 stalk of cleaned diced leek

Place brisket into a heavy dutchoven or iron roaster and cover with boiling water. Add above ingredients. Cook on top of stove until tender, usually 2 1/2 hours. Strain liquid and place meat on hot platter. Follow directions for making caper lemon sauce as in the Poached Meatballs recipe, only using the above meat stock. Slice brisket, place on platter and pour gravy over meat. Garnish with chopped parsley.

Excellent with polish cabbage noodles or Spatzle. Use several pieces of carrots and leeks for garnish.

Trudie Seybold

Gefüllte Schwäbisch Maultaschen
(Schwabian Meat Pies)

Noodle Dough:

1 1/4 c. flour	1/2 t. salt
2 eggs	4-5 T. water

Filling:

1/2 lb. lean pork	1/4 lb. beef
1/4 lb. veal	1/2 c. ice cubes

Grind above filling ingredients in food processor until fine.

Saute:

3/4 c. of smoked pork, diced	Pepper and salt to taste
1/2 c. croutons	1/2 t. nutmeg
1/2 c. green onions	2 cloves of garlic, minced
2/3 c. spinach, drained and chopped	Pinch of sugar

Simmer above for 10 mins.

Roll out dough and make 4" circles. Fill each and egg wash edges. Place in a kettle with 1 c. of soup broth and simmer until done.

Can be sliced and added to clear soup. Garnish with minced chives. You can also saute them in an iron skillet with 1/2 melted butter.

Grind above filling ingredients in food processor until fine.

Tauben Quelle and Roland Bosch, Stuttgart, West Germany

Königsberger Klöpse
(Poached Meatballs In Lemon-And Caper Sauce)

Meatballs:

T. onions	1/3 lb. lean boneless veal
1/2 c. onions, chopped	(All meats should be ground together 3 times)
2 slices fresh white bread, remove crust	
2 T. heavy cream	3 flat anchovy fillets, drained, rinsed, and coarsely chopped or 1 t. anchovy paste
1/3 lb. lean boneless beef	
1/3 lb. boneless pork	2 T. finely minced parsley

2 eggs, lightly beaten

1/2 t. finely grated lemon rind

1/2 t. salt

1/4 t. freshly ground black peppers

Melt butter in small sacue pan over mod. heat and saute onions for 5 minutes, until transparent, but not brown. Remove from heat. Tear bread into small pieces into a large bowl. Add cream and mix well. Add onions, ground meat, anchovy paste, parsley, eggs, lemon rind, salt and pepper. Knead vigourously with hands until ingredients are well combined. Moisten your hands with cold water and shape mixture into 8 large meatballs, or small ones, if used as appetizers.

Poaching Liquid

2 qts. water

1 med. onion, peeled and pierced

1 whole clove

1 sm. bay leaf

1 t. salt

In heavy 8 qt. sauce pan or soup pot, bring water to boil. Add onions, bay leaves, salt and boil uncovered for 10 min. Reduce heat to low and drop in meatballs. Simmer uncovered for 20 min., or until the Klopse rise to the surface of the water. With slotted spoon, transfer Klopse to a deep heated platter and cover. Strain liquid.

Sauce:

4 T. butter	1 T. capers, drained
4 T. flour	2 egg yolks
3 T. fresh lemon juice	2 T. sour cream

In heavy 10" skillet, melt butter over moderate heat. Stir in flour, 3 c. poaching liquid and bring to a boil, beating constantly with a whisk until the sauce thickens and is smooth. Reduce heat to low. Add lemon juice and capers. Simmer uncovered, stirring constantly.

In a small bowl, break the egg yolks up with a fork and stir in 1/4 c. simmering sauce. Whisk the mixture back into the skillet and stil in sour cream. Taste for seasoning. Add meatballs and simmer, basting from time to time until they are thoroughly heated. Serve with boiled potates and a green salad.

Trudie Seybold

Brisket of Beef

3-4 lb brisket of beef

1 pkg. Lipton's onion soup

1 lrg. diced clove of garlic

salt and peper to taste

6 whole cloves

1/2 c. dark brown sugar

Using heavy duty foil, place brisket in center. Add onion soup, garlic, and spike the beef with whole cloves and add brown sugar. Wrap tightly and close all ends. Bake in moderate over (325 degrees) for approx. 4 hours.

Slice thin and serve with buttered noodles.

Char-Grilled London Broil

4-5 lbs. London broil	1/2 c. dry vermouth
1 onion, diced	1/4 c. pure olive oil
1 lrg. clove of garlic, diced	2 t. crushed oregano leaves

Mix above ingredients together and pour over meat. Marinate overnight in refrigerator or 4 hours at room temperature.

Grill and serve.

Trudie Seybold

Beef Rouladen

4 thin slices top round (trim fat and pound with tenderizer mallet).

Mixture:

Saute the following in melted butter,

1/2 c. chopped mushrooms	1 c. diced ham or chopped cooked bacon
1/2 c. chopped onions	
1/2 c. diced celery	2 cloves of garlic, pressed
	1/2 c. chopped dill pickles or whole spears

Saute until tender. Add salt, pepper and 1 t. garni bouquet herbs.

Take a small amount of prepared mustard and spread over each piece of meat. Place 1/4 of mixture in center of each steak. Roll and fold together and fasten with toothpicks. Blanch each roll in flour. Melt butter in heavy iron skilled and saute until nice and brown. Remove rolls and add in skillet:

2 T. flour

1 c. bouillon

1 sm. diced onion

1 chopped carrot

Salt and pepper

Stir until gravy is nice and smooth. Add 1 t. Worcestershire sauce. Place rolls in heavy baking pan with cover and pour gravy over rouladen and cover. Bake in moderate oven (325 degrees) for 1 hour. Add 1 c. burgundy wine and 1 c. chopped mushrooms. Bake 1/2 hour longer or until tender. Serve with sprinkled parsley and Spatzle. Serves 4

Kurt Seybold

Memminger Meat Pie

Crust:

1 c. flour

7 oz. ricotta cheese

7 oz. butter

Pinch of nutmeg

Pinch of salt

Mix above in food processor and chill dough for approx. 2 hours.

Roll out into quiche type baking dish.

Filling:

1 lb. of rump steak, cut into strips

2 T. butter

Flour for blanching

1 minced onion

1 minced garlic clove

2 T. au jus gravy

1/2 lb. champeon or mushrooms

Salt & pepper to taste

1/2 c. heavy cream

Saute meat. add onion and other ingredients, adding cream last.

Pour meat mixture into crust and make a top, seal adding air holes. Bake at 400 or until golden brown. Serves 6.

Nina Sauter, Heimerdingen, West Germany

Salisbury Steak

2-3 lbs. round steak

1 lrg. diced onion

2 minced garlic cloves

1/4 c. diced carrots

Flour for blanching

1/4 c. minced parsley

1/2 c. sliced mushrooms

1/2 c. sour cream

2 sm. tomatoes, cut

1 t. summer savory

1 t. thyme

2 T. instant beef bouillon

1/2 c. soup stock or water

1 T. Worcestershire sauce

1/2 stick butter

Trim all fat and bone from round steak. Place between two pieces of wax paper and pound until thin with meat mallet. Heat butter and blanch beef until brown on both sides.

Add spices, onions, carrots, parsley, boullion soup stock, tomatoes, Worcestershire sauce, salt and pepper to taste.

Gravy should be nice and thick. If more thickness is desired, add more flour roux. Add mushrooms and sour cream. Let simmer until meat is tender. Serve and garnish with chopped parsley.

Delicious with buttered noodles or home made mashed potatoes.

Jennie Klose

Cuban Roast Pork

3 lbs. pork shoulder or fresh ham

Season with salt and pepper

1/3 c. lime juice or sour orange juice

1 lrg. onion, sliced

1/2 t. oregano

1/2 t. cumin

3 whole garlic cloves

Spear pork with garlic, mix marinade and pour over pork. Marinate for at least 1 day or overnight would be better.

Roast in oven, 35-40 min. per pound.

Luciano Moral, Augusta, KY

Pork Schnitzel

1 1/2 lb. pork tenderloin, trim, and cut crosswise into 12 slices, pound thin and place between 2 sheets of moistened wax paper for seasoning with salt and pepper for dredging.

3 lrg. eggs or egg scramblers, beaten until frothy

2 c. fine dry bread crumbs or Cornflake crumbs

1/2 c. finely chopped fresh parsley leaves

1/2 c. vegetable oil

115

For garnish:

3 hard-boiled large eggs, the white and yolks separated and minced fine

12 flat anchovy fillets, halved lengthwise

Lemon slices

Take one slice of pork, dredge in flour and dip into eggs, then into bread crumbs with parsley. In a large skillet, heat 2 T. of oil until fat is hot, but not burning. Saute the pork in batches, burning it and adding the remainder of the oil for 4 min. Transfer the pork onto a heated platter. Sprinkle the yolks and white over the pork, criss-cross 2 anchovy strips on top of each slice and arrange the lemon slices decoratively on the platter. Serves 6-8.

Trudie Seybold

Pork Tenderloin

2 avg. pork tenderloins

1/2 c. flour

1 t. salt

Cooking oil for frying

1/2 c. chopped onion

1 c. consomme

1 c. mushroom slices with juice

1 c. red wine

1/2 c. chopped green olives

1/2 c. chopped ripe olives

1/2 c. slivered almonds

Cut tenderloins in slices, pound thin, shake in bag with flour and salt. Brown meat in skillet. Remove meat and add onion to skillet and brown lightly. Add consommé, mushrooms, juice, red wine, olives and almonds. Stir and heat.

Arrange meat in oblong casserole, pour mixture over and mix through meat and cover. Bake 1 hr. 15 min. at 350 degrees. Remove cover the last 15 min. Serves 8.

Fritzie Heidt

Pork Tenderloin in Sour-Cream Paprika Sauce

3/4 c. finely chopped onion

1/2 c. finely chopped green bell pepper

5 T. butter

1 garlic clove, minced

1/2 lb. thinly sliced mushrooms

1 T. flour plus flour seasoned with salt and pepper for dredging the pork

4 t. Hungarian paprika

2 T. tomato paste

1 t. Worcestershire sauce

1 T. lemon juice

1/3 c. dry white wine

1/2 c. chicken stock

1 1/2 lbs. pork tenderloin, trim and cut crosswise into 12 slices, pound thin.

2 T. vegetable oil

3/4 c. sour cream

In a heavy kettle, cook onions and pepper in 4 T. butter until vegetables are softened. Add garlic and cook mixture for 1 min. Add mushrooms and cook for 3 mins. Stir in 1 T. flour and cook mixture. Stir in paprika and cook mixture. Mix in Worcestershire sauce, lemon juice, wine, tomato paste, and broth. Bring mixture to a boil and simmer for 3 min. Season with salt and pepper to taste.

Dredge the pork strips in seasoned flour, shaking off excess flour. In a large skillet, heat oil with remaining 1 T. butter over mod. high heat until fat is hot. In fat, saute pork for approx.

6 min. In a small bowl, combine 1/2 c. mushroom mixture with sour cream, whisking the mixture slowly back into the mushroom mixture in the pot. Stir in pork and any juices that have accumulat-

ed on the plate. Heat mixture thoroughly, but do not boil. Serve the pork mixture on a large platter with noodles. Serves 6.

Egg noodles, tossed with melted butter and caraway seeds is a delicious accompaniment.

Trudie's Gourmet Collectibles

Roast Pork Mit Kraut

3 lb. pork roast	Lrg. pkg. fresh sauerkraut
1 lrg. onion	Sugar to taste
Salt and pepper to taste	Lrg. apple

Boil pork roast in lrg. pot with water, onion, salt and pepper for approx. 1 hr.

Remove and place pork roast in a roasting pan in oven until desired tenderness.

Put sauerkraut in juice water from pork and cook on low until pork is ready to be served. Add a pinch of sugar, if a sweeter kraut is desired.

Slice pork and put on platter with sauerkraut. Serve with applesauce.

Boo Rehling, Cincinnati, OH

Chicken and Dumplings

1 stick butter (1/4 lb.)	1 celery stalk
1 4 1/2 lb. chicken (cut in pieces)	1 t. peppercorns
1 med. onion, finely grated	Salt and freshly ground pepper to taste
2 qts. stock or water	Chopped fresh parsley

Melt butter in a large heavy kettle with a cover. When butter is hot, but not brown, add chicken pieces, dark meat first. Sprinkle in grated onion and turn chicken pieces frequently, being careful not to let them stick or burn. When pieces are seared, pour in eough stock to cover them. Add celery and peppercorns. Cover pot and simmer until chicken is tender, approx. 1 1/2 hours. When chicken is cooked, remove pieces to a warm platter and cover with foil. Strain stock, discarding peppercorns, celery and bits of onion. Wipe pot clean and return the broth to the pot. Salt and pepper to taste. Remove skin from chicken pieces and add to pot.

Dumplings:

2c. all purpose flour	1 t. sugar
1/4 t. salt	1/2 lb. unsalted butter
2 t. baking powder	2/3 c. milk

Sift flour, salt, baking powder and sugar together in a med. size bowl. Cut butter into small pieces and add it to flour mixture. Blend it in quickly with your fingertips. Add milk and mix thoroughly, but do not overmix.

On a lightly floured surface, roll the dough to a 1/4" thickness. Cut into 1 1/2" round dumplings. Put in pot and simmer for 20 min. covered. Serve immediately.

Jessie Black, Cincinnati, OH

119

Chicken Paprika

Cut up as for frying:

A young chicken, about 2 1/2 lbs. plus 2 whole chicken breasts.

Melt in a heavy dutch oven pot:

1 1/2 T. butter   1 1/2 T. cooking oil

Add and simmer until golden:

1 1/2 c. chopped onions   2 1/2 T. sweet Hungarian
                                   paprika

Add:

1/2 t. salt   2 c. well-seasoned stock

As soon as these ingredients have reached the boiling point, add the chicken. Simmer covered until tender, about 1 hour.

Stir 1 t. flour into 1 c. cultured sour cream. Stir in slowly into pot. Heat the chicken 5 minutes longer, but do not boil. Serve at once.

Good served with buttered spatzle.

Carolann and Jim Slouffman, Cincinnati, OH

Pecan Apple Stuffing

1 loaf white bread, cubed	2 t. marjoram
1 c. soup stock	1 t. sage
1 onion, chopped	Salt and pepper to taste
1/2 c. minced parsley	1/2 lb. pork sausage
4 lrg. cooking apples, diced	1 stick margarine or butter
1 c. celery, diced	1/2 c. pecans

Soak bread in hot soup stock and set aside. Saute remaining ingredients in melted butter in large skillet until celery and onions are tender.

Mix in bread cubes - add more bread if mixture is too thin. Bake in casserole dish or stuff chicken or turkey. Serves 4.

Trudie Seybold

Rock Cornish Hens

1 box Uncle Ben's Brown and Wild Rice

2 qts. of stock or water

4 lrg. rock cornish hens

4 livers

1 sm. onion

1/4 lb. margarine

2 celery stalks

Sm. bunch parsley

Salt and white pepper to taste

2 t. marjoram

1 jar of orange marmalade

Bring soup stock to a boil and add rice as directed on the box.

In food-processor, add livers, onion, parsley, celery marjoram, salt and pepper. Saute the above ingredients in margarine until tender. Cook rice until all stock has been used. Mix with onion mixture.

Dry inside of hens and rub with marjoram. Fill each hen and overlap skin. Brush each hen with melted margarine and orange marmalade. Bake at 375 degrees for approx. 1 1/2 hrs. or until brown and done. Baste several times while baking. Serves 4.

Alternate recipes

1/2 c. seedless grapes, peeled

1/2 c. slivered almonds

Trudie Seybold

Marinaded Forest View Gardens Duck

6 duck breasts or 4 lb. whole duck (duck breasts are the most wonderful item)

1 c. dry sherry

1/2 c. soy sauce

1 lrg. onion, diced

2 cloves garlic, pressed

2 T. grated fresh ginger root

2 bay leaves.

Marinate duck breasts for at least 2 days in refrigerator.

These breasts are delicious for a cook-out. Grill and baste until med. well. Serve on a bed of wild rice.

Luciano Moral, Augusta, KY

Braised Veal Shank

7-8 lbs. meaty veal shanks, cut through bone, into 3" thick slices

All purpose flour

1/2 c. margarine, oil or butter

1 1/2 c. dry white wine

2 lrg. onions, minced

2 carrots, cut into 1/2" pieces

5 sprigs parsley

1 c. chicken broth

2 T. au jus base

3 cloves crushed garlic

1 t. bouquet garni

1 1/2 T. grated lemon rind and slivers of lemon for garnish

Salt and pepper to taste

Sprinkle veal with salt and pepper and roll in flour. Melt butter in heavy 8 qt. kettle over med. heat. Add some of the veal and brown on all sides. Remove and set aside. Add vegetables and brown (do not burn). Add some flour, wine, spices and broth to kettle. Return meat and bring to a boil. Cover and reduce heat and simmer until meat is very tender, when pierced and pulls from the bones. Approx. 1 to 1 1/2 hours.

Combine parsley, lemon peel, garlic and set aside. With a slotted spoon, remove meat to a warm platter. Keep warm. Run gravy through a foley food mill, skim and discard fat from sauce and bring to a boil over a high heat, stirring to loosen browned bits. Add parsley mixture and simmer until parsley is wilted. Pour sauce over the meat and garnish with remainder of parsley mixture. (Add au jus paste after food mill is processed).

Trudie Seybold

Marinaded Veal Cutlets

6 veal cutlets (see note*)	1 carrot, sliced very thin
2 eggs	1 clove of garlic, peeled and lightly crushed
1 1/2 c. unflavored bread crumbs	
	3 t. rosemary leaves
1/2 veg. oil	3 t. sage leaves
5 T. butter	3 bay leaves
3 T. olive oil	2 whole back peppercorns
1 c. onion, sliced very thin	1/2 c. water Pinch of salt

Beat eggs in a deep dish. Place the veal between two layers of wax paper and flatten with a meat pounder. Dip veal into beaten eggs. In another deep dish, put the break crumbs, salt and pepper. Mix well. Lifting one cutlet at a time, coat both sides with the bread crumbs. In a large saute pan, put the oil and butter and turn to med. heat. When the butter foam begins to subside, add the cutlets and cook until golden brown, turning once. Transfer to a paper towel to drain.

In a sauce pan, heat the olive oil to med. heat. Add onion, carrots, garlic, rosemary, sage, bay leaves, salt and pepper. Cook until onions turn transparent, about 10 min. Add the water-vinegar mixture, bring to a boil and cook 10-15 min.

Pour the hot marinade over the overlapping veal cutlets in a deep serving dish and discard the bay leaves and whole peppercorns. Let cook, cover and refrigerate for at least 12 hours. Serve room temperature. Serves 4.

*Skinned-boned chicken breasts or fish fillets may be substituted.

Inelda Tajo, Cincinnati, OH

Paprika Schnitzel

4 lrg. veal cutlets, cut thin

Flour for blanching

1 stick butter

3/4 c. onion, finely sliced

1 T. Hungarian paprika

1 T. instant beef bouillon (dissolved in 1/4 c. hot water)

Pepper to taste

1/2 c. sour cream

Prepare the veal as in previous recipes for German schnitzels. Melt butter in a heavy iron skillet. Blanch veal in flour and brown lightly on both sides. Add onions and bouillon. Saute for approx. 8 min. Stir in sour cream and paprika. Add salt and white pepper to taste. Serve immediately.

Garnish with chopped parsley.

Trudie Seybold

Lemon Sole Meuniere

4 8-10 oz. lemon sole fillets

1/2 c. butter

1/2 c. chopped parsley

1/4 c. fresh lemon juice

1 egg and 1/4 c. milk (for egg wash) beat together

Pat dry lemon sole, blanch on both sides in flour and dip into egg wash. Return to flour and coat both sides. In a heavy iron skillet, melt butter over med. high heat. When butter is hot, BUT NOT BURNING, place upper side of fish down. Lightly brown on both sides, sprinkle parsley over fish and add fresh lemon juice. Carefully life out of skillet with a spatula and place on plate.

This fish is very delicate and will tear easily.

Ladle a spoonful of lemon parsley butter on each serving. Garnish with parsley and slivers of fresh lemon.

Trudie Seybold

Thomas Hammons'
"One Eye'd Egyptians"
or
"Un Egyptien Avec Un Oeil"

Upon awakening to the lovely sounds of yellow finches entertaining themselves in your birdbath, having slipped gently from the duck designed flannel sheets (gently mind you so as not to disturb the Beloved slumbering still) and having performed one's morning (or afternoon) ablutions, proceed from your suite into the sunshine, breathe deeply and bend over, legs straight, to retrieve from your freshly mown lawn the latest Manchester Guardian.

Once in one's kitchen (having given your manservant the entire day off), produce from the ice box two (2) farm fresh eggs, two (2) really big pieces of white bread and a bit of unsalinated butter.

Place the bit of butter in a large cast iron skillet and, over a smallish flame, allow it to melt. At this point one may reminisce the previous evening's festive feast, the curl in the Beloved's upper lip having just sipped from your very best crystal a fine port by a rather roaring fire and her giggle as she pointed to the grey spats, which you just now notice are still on your feet. Sans-sock sans-shoe.

Discard now the smoking butter.

This matin's culinary delight having now your attention in toto, place another bit of butter in the recently cleansed skillet. Obtain a little metal lid (a grey poupon is just fine) and center it directly over each piece of bread. Keeping the better part of your man muscle in reserve, press in a downward direction so as to form a circular cutout. Lift the lid and detach the round form from inside. Repeat on the other slice. Both slices now being de-centered, gingerly place all four (4) pieces into the browned butter.

Commence singing Leporell's "Madamina" at a nice clip and proceed to your garden in order to obtain a rose exquisite enough to match the American Beatuy now clutching her pillow in your absence. Failing to accomplish this, notice one's neighbor's roses being decidedly better cultivated than your own and with all stealth (singing "ppp") detach quickly his finest. Run even quicker back into your kitchen, ignorning

-Hey you. Jerk, and the flying rake.

Having cracked a little on "d'ogni eta" (it *is* still early for a high e), turn each piece over and crack your farm fresh eggs into each newly created hole, the yolks thus forming the ocular element of this dish. Sing loudly enough to intimidate the neighbor, whose own voice now threatens to disturb the slumbering Beauty. Place the rose on a white wicker breakfast tray.

Grab one's most revered silver goblet and disrobing one's silken morning attire, ascent the steps to the roof of your mansion, raise your arms in the air and, buck naked, begin to sing Mephisto's "Le veau d'or est toujours debout". Just the first verse, though, or your breakfast will be ruined.

Run back to your kitchen just in time to remove this classic meal from the skillet and place it with great care on your Columbia enamel Wedgewood next to the rose.

Creep softly into your bedchamber and standing by the bed, sing with all the admiration your heart can muster, in your very best Lanza.

-Be my love and...

-Good Lord. What are those.

-Spats, dearest.

-Huh? Is that food?

-Not just food, my Beauty. One-eyed Egptians.

-Are those sirens?

-What? Oh...

-Hey. Who are you anyway?

Aim each piece of bread so that the semi-soft yolks connect with each of this trollop's eyes. Dress Hastily.

Drive to a finer hotel noted for it's breakfasts.

Rittenhouse Swim Club Blintzes

1 or 2 eggs	1 c. milk
1 c. flour	Pinch of salt

Make a smooth batter. Grease heated griddle or crepe pan. Pour in 2 T. batter. Make thin pancakes on one side only. Turn out on board or cloth towel. Cooked side facing up.

Filling:

Beat 2 eggs, frothy	Pinch of salt
Sugar to taste	1 T. flour to bind 8 oz. cream cheese

Blend above together.

Take pancake and place filling in middle, fold like an envelope and fry on both sides. Serve with sour cream and fresh berriesl

Hmmmmmmmmmm good!

Trudie Seybold

Hasenpfeffer

2 rabbits, cut into serving pieces.*

Marinade in:

2 c. water	1 med. sliced onion
2 c. vinegar	1 t. pickling spices (add a few peppercorns and bay leaves)
1/2 c. sugar	Marinate for 24 hours.
2 t. salt	

To Prepare:

Coat rabbits in flour and brown in cooker. To browned rabbits, add 1 c. of marinade. Process 15 min. in pressure cooker and remove rabbits. Add extra marinade and ginger snaps (crushed) to pressure cooker to make the gravy.

* If using wild rabbits, soak first in salt water for 24 hours. Rinse and then marinate.

Fay Fischesser Reading, OH

Grand Rack of Lamb or Veal With Grand Marnier

2 1 1/4 lb. trimmed and frenched single racks of lamb

7-8 ribs (you could also use 4-5 veal chops)

2/3 c. minced shallots

1/3 c. Grand Marnier

1/2 c. dry white wine

1/2 c. fresh orange juice

1 t. freshly ground black pepper

1 c. fresh or canned chicken stock

2 T. white vinegar

1 1/2 T. drained green peppercorns

2 T. blanched fine julienne of orange rind

8 T. cold unsalted butter, cut into pieces

In a skillet, brown the lamb, season with salt and pepper on all sides over mod. high heat. Bake the lamb or veal in a preheated 475 degree oven for 15-20 min. or until a meat thermometer registers 130 degrees for med. rare. Keep the lamb warm on a platter, covered.

Pour off all but one T. of fat from the skillet and add the shallots. Cook them until they are soft. Deglaze the pan with the Grand Marnier, wine and juice. Add black pepper, broth and vinegar. Boil mixture until it is reduced to 1 cup. Strain the mixture through a sieve into a sauce pan and add the green peppercorns and orange rind. Over low heat, whisk in the butter, one piece at a time and season the sauce.

Slice the rack and spoon the sauce over it. Serves 4

Trudie Seybold

Venison mit Cognac and Green Peppercorns

1 lb. thin sliced venison round steak

1 T. flour

1/2 c. butter

1 clove minced garlic

1/2 c. good cognac

1/2 c. beef stock

1/4 c. green peppercorns

1/4 c. sliced mushrooms

1/4 c. onions

Salt to taste

Marinade:

1/2 c. red burgundy wine

1/2 c. red wine vinegar

2 bay leaves

Few juniper berries

1 lrg. sliced onion

1 lrg. lemon juice and rind

1/2 c. olive oil

Make sure that you devein and clean venison steaks. Place in covered dish in refrigerator and marinate for 2-3 days.

Heat butter in heavy iron skillet. Blanch each steak in flour and brown on both sides. Add stock, salt, garlic, mushroom and onions. Let simmer for 10 min. Add cognac and ignite. Let flame cook off and add green peppercorns. Simmer another 5 min. or until tender. Serve immediately. Garnish with chopped parsley.

Delicious with Spätzles or Potato Dumplings.

Trudie Seybold

Kässe Spätzle
(Swiss Cheese Spätzle Casserole)

1 recipe of unwashed spätzle

1 1/2 lbs. firm good grade swiss cheese, grated

1 sm. onion

sliced thinly 1/2 stick butter

Delicious casserole eaten in Memmingen, Germany.

Use a deep dish casserole with a lid. Cook spatzle as explained in spatzle recipe. DO NOT RINSE spatzle. Alternate one layer of spatzles and one layer of cheese. Bake in a slow oven 325 degrees for approx. 20 min., until cheese is melted throughout the spatzles.

Melt butter in sauce pan and add sliced onion. Brown to a golden brown, not burned. After Spatzles are baked garnish with browned onions and serve immediately.

Kurt Seybold

Gaga Knox Corn Pudding

1 can of corn

Pinch of salt

2 T. sugar

1 lump of butter

1 c. cream

Stir above ingredients together and pour into greased casserole dish and bake at 350 degrees for 1/2 hr., or until set.

Hollywood Spaghetti

1 lb. box spaghetti	Salt and pepper to taste
3 lbs. lean ground beef	1/2 t. basil
1 chopped green pepper	1/2 t. oregano
3 cloves minced garlic	1 lrg. can of whole tomatoes
1 lrg. minced onion	1 lb. grated Cheddar cheese
1/2 lb. sliced mushrooms	1 qt. thick white sauce

Cut and cook spaghetti until tender and drain. Saute ground beef, green pepper, garlic, onion, salt, pepper, basil and oregano. Make a white sauce. See Sauces.

Alternate layers in a large casserole: white sauce, meat, mushroom, spaghetti, diced tomatoes, grated cheese and bake at 350 degrees until set. Approx. 1 1/4 hrs.

Laura Nestor, Wyncote, PA

Paella

Stock:

Shell from 1 doz. lrg. shrimp and 1 doz. mussels	4 c. water
1/2 lb. smoked pork	oregano, turmeric, salt to taste

Boil above ingredients, remove meat and strain liquid. Set aside.

2 T. olive oil	1 doz. scallops
3/4 lb. chorizo, casings removed, cut into 1/4" slices	1/4 c. cloves
	1 c. sherry wine
1 lrg. onion, chopped	1 pkg. (10 oz.) frozen artichoke hearts, thawed
1 red or green pepper; seeded and chopped	
	3 1/2 c. above stock
2 lrg. cloves of garlic, crushed	8 pieces chicken or just chicken legs
2 c. long-grain rice	
1/2 t. ground saffron	1 doz. shrimp
1/2 t. dry basil	Salt and pepper to taste

Sprinkle chicken with salt and pepper. Heat oil in a wide frying pan over med. high heat. Add chicken and cook, turning as needed, until well browned on all sides. Remove from pan and set aside.

Add sausage and cook until browned, remove and set aside. Discard all but 3 T. of pan drippings. Add onion, bell pepper and garlic to drippings. Cook, stirring until onion is soft. Add rice, saffron, basil and stir to coat rice with drippings. Transfer rice mixture to a wide shallow paella 4 qt. casserole. Arrange chicken, sausage and artichoke hearts over rice. Take 4 c. broth and bring to a boil and pour over rice mixture. Tightly cover casserole with foil or paella cover and bake in 350 degree oven for 30 min. Uncover and stir lightly to mix ingredients. Push shrimp into top of rice. Cover and bake 10 min. more or until shrimp turn pink. Uncover and push mussels into rice and scatter tiny peas (lobster tails if you wish) or 8 white asparagus and cover and bake for about 5 more min., or until mussels are heated through and all liquid is absorbed. Serves 6.

Luciano Moral, Augusta, KY

Bacon Onion Rolls

1/2 qt. chopped bacon	Seasoned salt
1 3/4 c. chopped onions	1 1/2 puff pastry (10x15x1/8")

Fry bacon until crisp. Remove bacon from drippings and drain on paper towel. Fry onion in bacon grease until golden brown. Remove onion with slotted spoon and drain on paper towel. Mix bacon, onions and season to taste with seasoned salt.

Cut each oblong of puff pastry in half, lengthwise, making 2-5x15" strips. Spread each strip with 6 T. bacon and onion mixture. Roll up like a jelly roll, starting at the 15" side. cut each roll into 12 pieces. Place pieces, seam side down on ungreased cookie sheet. Bake in preheated 425 degree oven for 15 min.

Trudie Seybold

Brussel Sprouts German Style

1 box fresh brussel sprouts	Salt and pepper to taste
1/4 stick butter or margarine*	1/2 t. sugar
2 T. flour	1/4 t. nutmeg
1 1/2 c. soup stock	2 cloves minced garlic
1 sm. diced onion	Pinch of baking soda

Place sprouts into boiling stock. Add onions, salt, pepper, sugar, nutmeg, garlic and simmer until tender. Add a pinch of baking soda to keep lovely green color.

In a sm. sauce pan, melt butter *(if on a diet, use WW chicken bouillon), over low heat and add flour to make a roux, adding liquid from sprouts; mixture will thicken. Serve hot and garnish with chopped parsley.

Mama Klose

Eggplant Parmigiana

1 lrg. eggplant, peeled and sliced into 1/4" slices	1 c. Italian seasoned breadcrumbs
Flour for dredging	4 oz. shredded Mozzarella cheese
2 T. olive oil	
1 egg, slightly beaten	Garnish with minced parsley and grated parmesan cheese
Marianta sauce	

Soak sliced eggplant in warm salted water, for approx. 15 min. Drain and pat dry with paper towels. Dredge each slice of eggplant in flour, dip in egg mixture and then coat both sides with seasoned breadcrumbs. Heat olive oil and fry each side of eggplant until golden brown.

Place each slice side by side in a shallow oblong baking pan. Top with Marianta sauce. Bake in mod. oven at 350 degrees for approx. 20 min. Top with Parmesan and Mozzarella cheese and return to oven and bake for 5 min. Serve immediately. Serves 4.

Variations: Veal, pork tenderloin, boneless skinless chicken breasts, scaloppini of turkey strips. Cooking time may vary somewhat.

Trudie Seybold

Stuffed Eggplant

4 sm. eggplants

2 1/2 c. fresh tomatoes, peeled and chopped *or* 1 #2 can solid-pack tomatoes

1 finely chopped onion

Herb-seasoned bread crumbs or prepared dressing mix

1 c. chopped celery hearts, including tops

1 t. basil

Butter or olive oil

Salt and pepper to taste

1/2 t. sugar

Select firm eggplants and wash well. Cut in half lengthwise, leaving stem if any. Using a curved grapefruit knife, cut out the center, leaving about 1/2" in the shell.

Butter the shells well and place them in a shallow baking dish or casserole containing about 1/2" water.

Cut centers of eggplant into small pieces and put in sauce pan, discarding any coarse seedy portion. Add celery, tomatoes, basil and seasonings. Saute onion in butter and add to mixture. Stir constantly until tender and mixture is thick.

Place mixture in shells, sprinkle with crumbs and dot generously with butter. Bake in 325 degree oven for about 15 min. Drain water from bottom of pan, garnish with thin slices of fresh tomatoes and a strip of broiled bacon on top of each serving. Serves 4.

Trudie Seybold

Polish Noodles and Cabbage

1/4 c. butter or margarine

1/2 c. chopped onion

4 c. chopped or sliced cabbage

1 t. caraway seeds

1/2 t. salt

1/8 t. white pepper

1 pkg. (8 oz.) egg noodles

1/2 c. sour cream (optional)

Melt butter in large skillet, add onion; saute until soft. Add cabbage, saute 5 min. or until crisp-tender. Stir in caraway seeds, salt and pepper.

Meanwhile, cook noodles in salted boiling water as directed on package. Drain well.

Stir noodles into cabbage. Add sour cream, if desired. I like it better without the sour cream. Cook 5 min. longer, stirring frequently. Serves 6-8.

Trudie's Collectibles

Bacon & Cheddar Souffleed Stuffed Tomatoes

2 russet or Idaho baking potatoes, about 1/2 lb. each (scrub and rub with vegetable oil)

3 T. unsalted softened butter

2 T. milk

1/8 t. cayenne pepper or to taste

3 T. minced scallions

3 large eggs, separate the whites at room temperature

5 slices lean bacon, cooked until crisp, drained and crumbled

1 1/4 c. coarsely grated cheddar cheese

Prick potatoes a few times with a fork and bake in 450 degree oven for 1 1/2 hr. Let potatoes cool for 15 min., halve them and scoop them out leaving crisp shells. Place potatoes in mixer, add butter, milk, cayenne pepper and scallions. Combine the mixture well, and stir in egg yoks.

In another bowl, beat the egg whites until stiff peaks form and add salt. Stir one third of the whites into the potato mixture with bacon and 1 c. of cheddar cheese. Fold in the remaining whites gently and divde the mixture among the potatoes shells.

Arrange the potatoes in a baking dish and sprinkle them with the remaining 1/4 c. cheddar cheese and bak in preheated 400 degree oven for 20 min. or until they are slightly puffed and set. Serves 4.

Trudie Seybold

German Pureed Spinach

2 pkgs. frozen chopped spinach

1 1/2 t. grandular chicken bouillon

1 sm. chopped onion

1 T. chopped parsley

1 clove minced garlic

1 T. flour

1 T. butter

Salt and white pepper to taste

1/2 c. heavy cream

Cover spinach with boiling water. Add onion, garlic and boil until spinach is completely thawed. Do not overcook. Drain all liquid. Place spinach in food processor using the puree knife.

In a heavy sauce pan, melt butter, flour and stir. Add heavy cream, chicken bouillon, parsley, salt and white pepper. Add the pureed spinach. If mixture is too thick, add more cream.

This dish can be prepared earlier, however, place sauce pan over boiling water or use a double boiler. Serve with chopped hard boiled eggs.

Mama Klose

Greek Spinach Pie

2 lbs. fresh or frozen spinach	1/4 t. nutmeg
3 eggs, lightly beaten	1 1/2 c. ricotta cheese
1 grated onion	3/4 lb. feta cheese
1 1/2 c. melted butter	1 pkg. Fillo dough
Salt and pepper to taste	

Boil spinach in very little water until thawed, drain. In a bowl, add spinach, eggs, 3/4 c. butter, onion, salt, pepper and nutmeg. Mix in ricotta cheese and crumble feta cheese.

Take a deep dish 9x12 pan and grease sides with butter. Open fillo leaves, find half section and open lengthwise. Brush two sheets with butter, spread spinach mixture, alternate leaves with spinach. Make 8-9 layers. Brush each layer and top with butter. Work fast so that fillo leaves do not dry out. Score top of pie with sharp knife in triangles.

Bake at 375-400 degrees for 45 min., then increase oven to 475 degrees for another 5-10 min., until golden brown. Serve from pan while hot. (Instead of ricotta cheese, you may use cream cheese).

Trudie Seybold

Mock Acorn Squash
(Spaghetti Squash)

1 3 1b. spaghetti squash	Molly butter buds
Sweet and Low	1 box egg scrambler
Cinnamon	

Have your produce man cut the squash in half. Place the squash on a paper towel and place in microwave for approx. 30 min. Take out and remove seeds from center. Loosen the squash from the sides and spray with Weight Watchers butter, or add butter buds, cinnamon and sweet and low. Mix together.

For variation, add one box of egg scramblers (equivalent to 2 egg whites) mix and place into oblong cake pan and bake for 20 min. in 350 degrees or until set. Last 3 min., broil the topping until golden brown.

Trudie Seybold

German Apple Pancakes

Oil	1/2 c. flour
2 lrg. Roman, Macintosh or Granny Smith apples, peeled and sliced 1/8" core	Pinch of salt
	1 t. sugar
	4 T. milk
1 egg	

Stir egg, flour, sugar, salt and milk together. Heat oil in heavy skillet. When hot, blanch each apple slice in egg batter and fry on low flame until each side is golden brown. Dust with powdered sugar. Serves 2-4 people.

Trudie Seybold

Austrian Gugelhupf

1 c. butter	6 eggs, separated
2 c. sugar	1 1/2 c. sifted flour

1/2 t. salt

6 T. milk

2 t. baking powder

Lemon rind or vanilla

Beat eggs separately. Cream butter and sugar together. Fold in eggs, flour, salt baking powder and vanilla. Bake in greased gugelhupf pan for 1 hr. and 10 min., at 350 degrees.

Trudie Seybold

Black Walnut Cake

1 lb. butter

1 lb. sugar

9 eggs, separated

1 lb. flour

1 lb. black walnuts (I use 1/2 lb. black walnuts, 1/4 c. pecans and 1/4 walnuts. The black walnut's taste is rather strong)

Cream butter and add sugar. Add egg yolk, one at a time. Add flour and nuts. Fold in stiff egg whites. Bake in a very deep well greased bundt pan Bake in slow over (275) for approx. 2 1/2 hrs.

Trudie Seybold

Carrot Cake

3 eggs

1/2 c. raisins

Pinch of salt

2 t. baking powder

1 1/2 c. sugar

1/2 c. chopped walnuts

2 c. cooked grated carrots

2 t. cinnamon

1 c. oil

2 t. vanilla

1/2 c. coconut

2 c. flour

Beat eggs until frothy. Add sugar and oil. Slowly add flour, baking powder and cinnamon, salt. Blend in carrots, coconut, raisins, walnuts and vanilla, by hand. Pour into greased cake pans and bake at 350 until set. Ice with cream cheese icing.

Trudie Seybold

German Cheese Cake Jennie's Style

6 eggs, slightly beaten	1/2 t. grated lemon rind
1 qt. cottage cheese	1/2 c. currants
1 c. sugar	1 pt. whipping cream
1/4 lb. butter or margarine	1 T. flour
8 oz. cream cheese	

Place cottage cheese, sugar, butter, cream cheese, flour and lemon rind in blender and mix until smooth. Fold this mixture slowly into the beaten eggs, currants and whipped cream.

Line a spring form pan with buttered, sugared graham cracker crumbs. Press crumbs on bottom of pan. Pour in cheese cake mixture and bake in a very slow oven (250 degrees) for approx. 1 hr. Let cake cool in oven. When cool, remove spring sides and chill.

Serve with fresh strawberries or blueberries and top with whipping cream.

In Loving Memory Of Jennie Klose

Trudie's Quick Cheese Cake

Preheat Oven to 350

With electric mixer, beat together 6 eggs until frothy and gets a thick lemon color. Slowly add 1 1/2 c. sugar and 1 T. lemon rind.

In a separate bowl, beat together 3 lbs, ricotta cheese, 12 oz. cream cheese, 1 1/2 c. sour cream, and 1/4 c. flour. Add 1 c. sugar and 2 t. vanilla and cream together WITH A WOODEN SPOON, THE EGG & CHEESE MIXTURE.

THIS CAN BE BAKED IN A SPRING FORM OR CAKE PAN 24x12x2

Crust:

Thickly grease bottom and sides of pan with melted butter or low-cal margarine.

Mix

1 1/2 c. graham cracker crumbs	1/2 c. sugar
	2 T. cinnamon

Dust the crumb mixture on the bottom and sides of pan. Pour in cheese and egg mixture and sprinkle with 1/4 c. of topping mix:

1 1/2 c. melted butter or margarine	1 1/2 c. crumbs
	1/2 c. sugar

Mix the above together and save crumbs for other cakes.

Trudie Seybold

Trudie's Sour Cream Cake

1 c. soft butter	1/2 t. salt
2 3/4 c. sugar	1/4 t. soda
6 eggs	1 1/4 c. sour cream
3 c. sifted flour	1 t. vanilla

This recipe can be made in a food processor. Preheat oven to 350 degrees. Grease and flour a 10" bundt pan. Cream butter with sugar, using mixer or processor. Add eggs, one at a time, beating well after each egg. Sift flour with salt and baking soda. Add flour to butter mixture in three batches alternately with sour cream. Blend in vanilla. Pour batter into prepared pan. Bake until top is light brown, approx. 11/4 hrs. Cool cake completely in pan before serving. Dust with powdered sugar.

Nut and Honey Cake

2 eggs	Pinch of salt
1/2 c. sugar	3/4 t. baking powder
1/4 c. brewed coffee	1/2 t. baking soda
1 c. honey	1 c. hazel nuts
1 T. salad oil	2 T. cognac
2 c. cake flour	

Beat eggs gradually and add the sugar, coffee, honey and oil, etc. Oil a 10" loaf pan and line it with wax paper or aluminum foil. Bake until done.

Trudie Seybold

Gaga Knox "Jam Cake"

1 c. butter	4 c. flour
1 1/2 c. raspberry jam	2 1/2 c. sugar
5 eggs	1 t. cinnamon, cloves, allspice and nutmeg
1 c. buttermilk	1 1/2 t. soda

Cream butter. Add sugar, raspberry jam with seeds and spices. Add one egg at a time and beat. Set buttermilk with soda aside. Add 2 c. flour, buttermilk and remaining flour and a pinch of salt. Bake in 2 greased 9" cake pans at 350 degrees.

Icing:

In a heavy sauce pan add 1 lb. box brown sugar, 1 c. white sugar, 1 lump of butter and 1 c. of milk. Cook until it makes a soft ball when dropped in cold water. Beat when cooled and ice cooled cake.

Churros
(Cuban Funnel Sweets)

1/2 c. milk	1 c. flour
1/2 c. water	1 egg

Beat the above ingredients together. Find an old funnel and drop into heated grease. Roll in sugar or powdered sugar.

Luciano Moral, Augusta, KY

Thanks for all the memories!
From Trudie, Kurt and Leo

CPSIA information can be obtained
at www.ICGtesting.com
Printed in the USA
FFOW02n0250230917
40228FF